IN GREAT TASTE

IN GREAT TASTE

FRESH, SIMPLE RECIPES
FOR EATING AND LIVING WELL

EVELYN H. LAUDER

FOUNDER AND CHAIRMAN, THE BREAST CANCER RESEARCH FOUNDATION
AND SENIOR CORPORATE VICE PRESIDENT, THE ESTÉE LAUDER COMPANIES

RODALE

Rodale books may be purchased for business or promotional use or for special sales. For information, please write to: Special Markets Department, Rodale Inc., 733 Third Avenue, New York, NY 10017.

Printed in the United States of America
Rodale Inc. makes every effort to use acid-free ♾, recycled paper ♻.

The Waldorf Chocolate Mousse recipe on page 206 is used with permission from Jean-Claude Perennou and the Waldorf-Astoria Hotel.

Interior photographs by Beatriz da Costa, except for those on pages 21, 57, and 135, which are © Evelyn H. Lauder

Book design by Marysarah Quinn

Library of Congress Cataloging-in-Publication Data

Lauder, Evelyn H.
    In great taste : fresh, simple recipes for eating and living well / Evelyn H. Lauder.
        p.   cm.
    Includes index.
    ISBN-13 978–1–59486–553–4 hardcover
    ISBN-10 1–59486–553–1 hardcover
    1. Cookery (Natural foods)   2. Menus.   I. Title.
TX741.L38 2006
641.5'63—dc22   2006023821

Distributed to the trade by Holtzbrinck Publishers

2   4   6   8   10   9   7   5   3   1   hardcover

We inspire and enable people to improve their lives and the world around them
For more of our products visit **rodalestore.com** or call 800-848-4735

Firstly, to Leonard, who delights in enjoying fine food.
Secondly, to my children and grandchildren, whom I love to feed.
Thirdly, to the memory of my grandmother, Rose; mother, Mimi;
and mother-in-law, Estée, for their influence on my palate.
Lastly, to all the dedicated colleagues at The Breast Cancer
Research Foundation, without whom the science would
never have moved forward so quickly.

CONTENTS

FOREWORD

In medical school I was taught that if I approached life properly, all of my experiences would make me a better doctor. The most meaningful experiences, of course, involve human relationships, and of these my friendship with Evelyn Lauder has been one of the most positive. Being scientific director of The Breast Cancer Research Foundation, the organization she founded in 1993, has permitted me to participate in the support of some of the most accomplished biomedical scientists as they have made concrete advances against this collection of diseases. As medical director of the Evelyn H. Lauder Breast Center at Memorial Sloan-Kettering Cancer Center in New York, I have been able to join with extraordinary colleagues to "push the envelope" in breast cancer prevention, detection, and care toward greater standards of excellence. Neither of these opportunities would have been possible without Evelyn's insight, engagement, leadership, and encouragement.

But perhaps Evelyn's greatest contribution to my own personal journey has been the inspiration she has provided regarding an approach to life filled with curiosity, delight, style, and dynamic involvement with other people. Every aspect of her life is marked by a sense of discovery, of artistic merit, and of value to everyone around her. It is a contagious quality and a joy to behold. Nowhere is this more apparent than in her attitude toward, and talent in creating, wonderful meals: the ultimate social skill! These meals combine healthy eating with beautiful aesthetics and unforgettable conversation. You hold in your hands a book that captures some of this magic, a guide not only to delicious adventures in food but also to a way of living that is pleasurable as well as productive. May your life, too, be enriched by this experience.

Larry Norton, MD

Medical Director, Evelyn H. Lauder Breast Center at Memorial Sloan-Kettering Cancer Center; Deputy Physician-in-Chief, Memorial Hospital (Breast Cancer Programs); Professor of Medicine, Weill College of Medicine, Cornell University; and Scientific Director, The Breast Cancer Research Foundation

ACKNOWLEDGMENTS

Tremendous thanks go to Sally Susman, whose idea it was to formalize into a book the recipes that had been created and cherished in my family. Jennifer Mann deserves credit for coordinating my schedule and keeping me focused on this project. Without Margaret Stewart I could not juggle any of my responsibilities in The Estée Lauder Companies' offices or, for that matter, anywhere. Margot Schupf's keen sense of editing for what is appropriate and relevant helped me to select from a wide variety of foods. Her knowledge of ingredients, marketing, design, and photography pulled all the elements together for me to be able to accomplish this labor of love. Without Darienne Sutton, food editor extraordinaire, the recipes would probably not have been tested with such a sure hand. Veronique Vienne assisted in pulling together all the parts of my ideas for the introduction. The renowned food photographer, Beatriz da Costa, has photographed each dish temptingly and dramatically, which pleases not only my eye but also hopefully that of each reader. The photos must also please Alison Attenborough very much since she is the creative food stylist whose plates are an accurate and attractive rendition of the recipes. The design and layout of this book were most creatively and artistically supervised by Marysarah Quinn, whose sense of color, style, and proportion are impeccable.

My special thanks to Heather Rodale and Rodale Inc. for initiating this project and for enthusiastically encouraging me to record my own and cherished family recipes for all to share.

Appreciation always to my good friend Dr. Larry Norton of Memorial Sloan-Kettering Cancer Center and scientific director of The Breast Cancer Research Foundation for taking time out of his extraordinarily busy schedule to write the foreword for this book. He teaches all of us about many things, including food. To the renowned Dr. Andrew Weil and to the well-known Elizabeth Hurley, my thanks for sharing their favorite delicious recipes for all to enjoy.

Lastly, to my husband, Leonard, whose patience with me during this effort even extended to him helping me in the kitchen, both in preparing our menus and in many, many other ways.

Evelyn H. Lauder
September 2006

IN GREAT TASTE

INTRODUCTION

Simple Pleasures, Healthy Rewards

I have always believed that health is the most wonderful of gifts. Health makes you look and feel vibrant and beautiful. Over the years, I have learned to cherish, protect, and celebrate this precious sense of wellness.

Doctors know that skin is a barometer of health; the doctor examines the color, temperature, and feel of the skin to judge wellness or discover illness. A healthy lifestyle combined with a healthy diet contributes to the radiance of your complexion. The role of skin-care products is to maintain—or restore—a healthy environment for your skin.

That's why, throughout my career as an executive in the beauty industry, I have made a point of meeting experts who are dedicated to solving health issues important to women. And because my rule of thumb is that a person should support worthy causes if she can, I have done my best to help these health-care professionals with their work by mobilizing fund-raising campaigns.

My involvement with breast health was prompted by a series of circumstances, the first being a resolution passed in 1988 by Congress making October "Breast Cancer Awareness Month." Organizations and individuals could raise awareness as they wished. At about the same time, the cosmetics industry started a program called "Look Good, Feel Better" to help female cancer patients overcome the skin and hair side effects of chemotherapy. This was in the late 1980s, when some women were so frightened at the prospect of losing their breasts—or their hair—that they didn't even get mammograms on a regular basis. They didn't know that breast conservation was being practiced in medical centers. This prompted me to help, as I wanted to reduce fear with knowledge.

Thanks to my editor friends in the beauty and health sections of magazines, articles about breast health began to appear in 1991. Until then, no one wrote about this subject. It touched a nerve with readers, who were grateful for information on the topic. Since then, almost every October, stories about breast health appear all over the world.

It was also during this period that I got started with the pink ribbon campaign, an idea first proposed by Alexandra Penney, then editor-in-chief of *Self* magazine, for her 1992 Breast Cancer Awareness Month issue. With the financial support of The Estée Lauder Companies (and my husband Leonard's personal underwriting commitment), I was able to take Alexandra's brilliant concept to the next level. That year, we painstakingly manufactured thousands of pink ribbons and distributed them free to our customers to encourage them to have mammograms and do regular self-examinations. It was a huge success. To this very day, we have distributed more than 60 million pink ribbons, and the Pink Ribbon has become ubiquitous as the worldwide symbol for breast health.

In 1990, I was flattered to be asked to join the Board of Overseers of the Memorial Sloan-Kettering Cancer Center. They were building a breast center, for which I dedicated 2 years to raising funds as well as ideas about how to make the center more efficient for the doctors and more convenient for the patients. When the center was completed in 1992, it became a model for other centers at Memorial Sloan-Kettering and for other hospitals around the country.

In 1993, realizing that there were very few coordinated efforts in breast cancer research, I felt compelled to initiate the formation of a new nationwide foundation to fill the need for research in breast health. I wanted to make sure my efforts were as effective as possible. So I started The Breast Cancer Research Foundation (BCRF), a not-for-profit charity that as of this book's publication supports more than 110 scientists worldwide, 97 in the United States and the remaining in Europe and South America. It has become almost a mini-institution, with the most creative physician researchers now in constant communication with each other. All of my proceeds from the sale of this book will be donated to the BCRF.

What I have learned about health through this process is both exciting and sobering. Exciting because new discoveries are constantly being made, sobering because we must proceed with care before jumping to conclusions. Indeed, as much as we all wish there were some definitive answers to the how-to-stay-healthy and how-to-prevent-illness questions, the jury is still deliberating, and no final verdict has been reached.

There is no official, FDA-approved correlation between what we eat and cancer prevention. Yet, certain truths are irrefutable. As the BCRF founder and chairman, and as a member of the Board of Overseers of the Memorial Sloan-Kettering Cancer Center, I am listening at the forefront of the latest research conducted by nutritionists and dietitians on this subject. I can vouch that all the findings point in the same direction: A diet rich in antioxidants and low in

RECENT FINDINGS

In 2005, a presentation was made at the annual meeting of the American Society of Clinical Oncology, based on the Women's Intervention Nutrition Study (WINS). This was a large-scale clinical trial of more than 2,400 postmenopausal women, supported by the National Cancer Institute and the BCRF. The study evaluated the effect of a low-fat diet on breast cancer recurrence and survival. Results showed that eating a low-fat diet reduced the risk of breast cancer recurrence by 20 percent over 5 years in postmenopausal women compared with women following a standard diet. The women in the study were breast cancer survivors who had had standard treatment (lumpectomy or mastectomy followed by radiation and then hormonal therapy or chemotherapy).

The take-home message therefore is: A large-scale study has demonstrated that if you are a postmenopausal woman who has had breast cancer and you follow a low-fat diet, you are decreasing your chances of recurrence.

saturated fat can make a difference. You can actively contribute to your health, and to the health of the people you love, by preparing simple meals at home and by eating smartly when you go out. Maintaining a healthy weight will also help prevent heart disease and diabetes, as well as knee and other joint problems.

Take my word for it: This collection of recipes is the reason I have so much energy and stamina. Each one of them is a tried-and-true favorite. As someone who is health-obsessed yet too busy to keep up with diet fads or fuss with complicated recipes, I have devised my own foolproof nutritional guidelines. We all know diets don't work, because they are temporary, and I believe that eating correctly becomes a way of life. From now on, when friends ask me, as they often do, how I manage to keep up with my hectic schedule and still look and feel good, I will simply give them this cookbook.

Morning, Noon, and Night

Eating, I believe, is about sustaining a sense of well-being throughout the day. At sunrise, you want to "break your fast" with small amounts of food rich in nutrients. Later, after 4 hours during which you have expended a lot of energy, you need a lunch that picks you up and keeps you going. Dinner, in contrast, should be light on your digestion yet deeply satisfying. Late-night noshing impulses, as pleasurable as they are once in a while, are not good for you on a regular basis.

The recipes are organized along this principle, to nourish you, energize you, or satisfy you, as the case may be. The three parts— Morning, Noon, and Night—are designed to help you enjoy preparing meals, serving them, and sharing them at all hours of the day. I like to think of sitting down for breakfast, lunch, or dinner as one of life's great pleasures.

To make sure that you have a really good time in the kitchen, I have also included quite a few of my personal tips. I believe that if you can do things correctly, you will gain a sense of control that will enhance your pleasure. Among the recipes, I have tucked in tip boxes on a wide range of topics, from how to choose ripe fruit to how to cut a lemon to how to chop herbs.

My hope is that whenever you decide to cook, with whatever ingredients you happen to choose, you always get the most out of the final result. After all, cooking for someone is an act of love.

Taste of Home

Why is a large and sunny kitchen usually the most popular room? No matter how small or grand a home, everyone is invariably drawn to the place where meals are prepared. I entertain in the dining room, but the kitchen is where I share lighthearted moments with family members, friends, and guests alike. Instinctively, we all know that it is where good things happen: where we can relax, let down our defenses, and experience the simple pleasures of easy conviviality. It is the heart of the house.

The same can be said of home-cooked meals. They not only bring us together, they are also the expression of our desire to care for each other, to provide wholesome sustenance to loved ones, and to contribute to the enjoyment and well-being of all those who are assembled.

As confusing as the information about health and nutrition seems at times, all experts agree on one thing: Eating *in* is more beneficial to our health than eating out.

The dishes that come out of your own kitchen do not contain as much hidden fat, sugar, salt, chemicals, and preservatives as dishes prepared commercially. The ingredients you use are probably fresher, the cooking methods simpler, the portions smaller, and the end product easier on your digestion. Although this is not a diet book, let me share this story with you: Last year, my husband was stuck at home as a result of a bad back. For about 3 weeks, we ate nothing but our own home-cooked meals. Both of us actually lost about 8 pounds. Leonard was so concerned that he went to see his doctor, because he had been eating hearty quantities during those weeks and was never aware of being denied any tasteful meals. Of course, there was nothing wrong with him.

Someday, we might find that the amount of time we spend in the kitchen is inversely proportionate to the amount of time we spend in doctors' waiting rooms! Meanwhile, we can rest assured that whenever we sit down to a home-cooked meal, we are doing something good for ourselves.

The Quest for Health

I am convinced that eating wholesome food at home does not have to be complicated or boring. In fact, it should be exciting. I refuse to think of making a healthy choice as "dieting"—such an overused word! Having nutritiously balanced meals is all about living life to the fullest.

To begin with, I make sure that meals are not routine events. I believe in having a change of scene. We eat different foods at different times of the day, and for different reasons, so why not eat in different places as well?

In the kitchen, one can sit down on high stools at the counter or on comfortable chairs at a nearby breakfast table. There is the option of the dining room for when we are in a more formal mood.

In our cabin in the country, there is a spot on the screened porch where in summer we can have breakfast or intimate suppers. Meanwhile, on cold nights, one can choose to settle down in front of a tray near the fireplace in the sitting room. And let's not forget picnics: We have a little red wagon, and weather permitting, we put our dishes in it, pile the food on top, and roll it down the hill to the picnic table set by the lake. When we are done, we roll the wagon back up with all the dirty dishes in it! Mind you, this particular house is a one-bedroom hideaway, yet there are at least four different places where we can set the table for a meal.

The only place where I do not like to eat is in bed! I hate the idea of having crumbs all over the sheets. On the other hand, having a cup of warm herbal tea in bed is pure bliss.

I am a firm believer that making the right choices is not only easy to start with, but it gets easier as you stick with it. Practically, once you get used to not eating certain things, you really don't miss them anymore. Avoiding harmful ingredients is not time-consuming. All you need to do is eliminate once and for all from your diet what's bad for you: the extra fat, the extra salt, and the extra sugar. As Dr. Larry Norton likes to say: "You only crave what you do eat. You don't crave what you don't eat." Larry is deputy physician-in-chief for breast cancer programs at Memorial Sloan-Kettering Cancer Center and is an expert when it comes to nutritional issues. He ought to know.

Unlike most cookbook authors, I do not have happy childhood food memories to serve as "appetizers" in this introduction. I grew up during World War II, a time of food shortages, and I do not think that there was a tremendous amount of fresh vegetables available anywhere. In those days, people bought a lot of canned vegetables. Frozen vegetables had yet to appear in the markets. Besides, as a child whenever I wanted to help my mother in the kitchen, she always said, "The best help to me is for you to stay out of the kitchen." When I was a child, I ate what my mother served, which was everything. However, I have fond memories of certain dishes my mother prepared regularly that I've scattered throughout this book. Only later in life did my mother become a follower of nutrition guru Gaylord Hauser, who was a proponent of eating fish and vegetables. Needless to say, as soon as I had my own kitchen, as a married woman, I began to experiment with the kind of food more likely to please the palate of a young husband. For the first time, I shopped for varieties of lettuce, for example—my mother loved only iceberg—and I learned to cook meat, roast beef in particular. Back then, you were considered a cheapskate if you served chicken when you had company.

When I was pregnant with my first child, my obstetrician insisted that I go on a no-salt diet to prevent swelling in my ankles.

It was a turning point when I discovered that I could use herbs and spices to add flavor to dishes, a practice I have adopted ever since. Getting rid of salt and developing instead a taste for tarragon, basil, thyme, rosemary, cilantro, lemongrass, turmeric, cumin, curries, sage, coriander, and oregano became a way of life for me, so much so that now I am always on the lookout for new herbs and spices to replace salt. As a fragrance "nose," the additional scent of these ingredients whets the appetite and adds something truly special to my meals.

Some time ago, while on a hike across the hills in Italy, I smelled something wonderful in the air—I thought that it was curry. Curry in Italy? No way. I followed this scented trail until I found on the side of the road a plant called "curry-rosemary," whose bouquet was simply enchanting. I took some home in the inside pocket of my jacket, and the smell lingered in my pocket for months afterward. Some time later, I read that both rosemary and curry, along with green tea and red grapes, happen to be some of the strongest antioxidants, and as such they are considered potent anticancer nutrients.

The Pleasure of the Senses

Planning a menu around something you can get only when it is in season is the most economical way to create a meal that is as tasty as it is healthy. Sometimes I buy exotic ingredients imported from faraway places, since today everything comes from other countries when it is out of season in our hemisphere, but I load my shopping cart with local delicacies and recently harvested fruits and vegetables when I can.

You can never go wrong with fruits, vegetables, and grains. They are a great source of antioxidants as well as a source of "phytochemicals"—substances possibly associated with the prevention of cancer, diabetes, cardiovascular disease, and hypertension. But they are beneficial to your health in other ways as well, as a source of fiber, vitamins, and natural oils. These oils are good for your skin. Many of the wonderful cleansing oils we use in the skin-care business are extracted from fruits, vegetables, and grains.

So there is no need to add butter to your vegetable dishes! You can enhance their taste without loading them up with cholesterol-friendly dressings. Circumventing butterfat forces one to be creative, and the results can be spectacular. Nothing is better—and healthier—than a baked potato topped with a mixture of fat-free sour cream, caviar, and a touch of lemon juice and sprinkled with chopped egg. Or what about sweet potatoes mashed with baked apples and spiced with amaretto? And I have yet to meet someone who does not rave when served my dish of mock snowflake "potatoes," a frothy mousse so light that it melts in your mouth—but made from cauliflower.

I am always careful to choose a recipe that brings out the taste of the food. For instance, I will marinate shrimp, chicken, or even steaks overnight. Or I will roast poultry the French way, very slowly at medium temperatures, to give it time to render its fat as well as absorb the flavor of its stuffing and the taste of the seasonings I rubbed into the cavity or on its skin.

Sometimes I combine searing with slow baking, such as when we occasionally eat roast beef. I place a beef roast in a very hot oven (500°F/260°C) for 20 minutes, long enough for a black crust to form on its surface. I then turn the oven off and let the trapped heat finish the job. This foolproof method (count 15 minutes per pound) produces sensational results: The meat is crusty on the outside, pink and tender on the inside. But do not open the oven door!

Color is also a concern when I am planning a menu. I would never serve fillet of sole with mashed potatoes or cauliflower au gratin—even though this bland-looking offering is delicious. Instead, I will grill the fish so that it acquires a crusty golden appearance, and I will serve string beans and carrots or yellow squash with it. The more colorful the plate, the more appetizing the food on it.

Texture is next: If one vegetable is chopped, the other should be pureed or creamed; if it is sliced, the other should be minced or hashed. For example, carrots cut on the diagonal are lovely with a broccoli puree and a paillard of turkey.

Setting the table nicely adds to the sensuous pleasure, and the food will even seem to taste better. Good lighting from candles and flowers on the table add visual pleasure to the fragrance of the dishes and the anticipation of dining in great taste.

One thing I never do is test a new recipe on unsuspecting guests. That's one rule of thumb: When you have company, don't attempt to prepare something that you have never made before. The instructions in your cookbook might not be compatible with the settings on your stove, the type of pots you use, or the skills of the cook.

Energy Treats

Home-cooked meals are healthy, but who am I kidding? No one has time to eat at home three times a day, seven days a week. More likely, one is eating on the run, munching and noshing all day long, with hardly any time for a proper lunch. I am no exception. Even though I am more disciplined than most when it comes to breakfast—I start the day with my yogurt drink or oatmeal or muesli—I depend on snacks to make it through the day.

I wish that I could tell you that I am always nibbling on carrot and celery sticks whenever I am hungry, but that's not the case. Like everyone else, I crave comfort food now and then. But in order not to succumb to the lure of chocolate chip cookies, I have a list of healthy "pick-me-uppers" that satisfy my nutritional needs as well as my sweet tooth.

Besides raw vegetables, I'll have a couple of rice or corn cakes with a tiny bit of jelly on them. They require so much chewing, I am not likely to have more than two! I also keep in my office a little bowl full of the prettiest cherry tomatoes—the sweet kind that are sold on the vine—and I pop them into my mouth as if they were candies on my way out the door to a meeting or an appointment. But one of my favorite snacks is a combination of almonds and dried California apricots. I take a small bite of an almond and an apricot at the same time, and together they taste like a scrumptious cookie. Six almonds and three apricots usually do the trick—the mixture of fruitiness and crunchiness is deeply satisfying.

Sipping on a warm beverage is another way to appease a mid-morning or midafternoon yen. You can nurse a cup of hot tea or a mug of steaming broth for 20 minutes as it cools down. Usually you feel full by the time you swallow the last drop.

Beware: The amount of sugar and fat in so-called health bars makes these snacks almost as fattening as old-fashioned candy bars. I once spent half an hour comparing the nutritional benefits of the various "energy" bars at my local grocery store and found that they contained on the average 250 calories from sugar and up to 10 grams of fat. All of that in a tiny little bar that you can polish off in less than 2 minutes.

It's simple: The more time it takes to consume a snack, the better it is for you. So, to eat an apple, slice carefully and place on a plate with a fork; or scoop half a container of yogurt into a small bowl and put a handful of raisins on top; or cut a piece of low-fat cheese into dainty little triangles. Arrange these treats on a pretty plate with a folded paper napkin on the side. Pleasure your eyes as much as your stomach. When you are hankering for something delicious, presentation makes all the difference.

Food for Thoughts

Ultimately, a healthy meal nourishes the body but also the mind. And I don't just mean that you must ingest the kind of nutrients that keep your neurons firing. No. A healthy meal is one during which you get to sit back, unwind, and share stimulating ideas with your dinner companions. But, let's face it, if you are the hostess, chances are your mind is preoccupied with serving the meal as much as partaking in the conversation. It's often a great treat to go out to dinner. Especially if you've had a full day, meeting friends for dinner gets you off your feet and relaxes you.

Going to a restaurant requires some preparation in order to resist the temptation of eating too much of the wrong thing—the hot buns, the sweet butter, the creamy salad dressing, the french fries, and the all-you-can-pile-on-your-plate buffet food. Because my social life and fund-raising work require me to be out and about town more often than I ever thought was humanly possible, I have tried to turn going out at night into a science.

Most detrimental are the late hours that we keep. By the time you sit down, you are starving, so you eat too much, too fast, and you tend to choose dishes that are too rich, calorie-wise. You do not get up from the table until 10 o'clock, barely an hour before bedtime. And if you go to sleep on a full stomach night after night, believe me, soon your evening gowns feel too tight.

Before getting dressed for dinner, at about six-thirty, I eat a fat-free yogurt or I munch on raw vegetable sticks, enough to take the edge off the pangs in my stomach. Hours later, after cocktails, while people around the table are eagerly perusing the menu for an entrée that matches the size of their ravenous appetite, I feel no such desperation and I am not likely to regret some foolish choices later.

Most of the time, though, restaurant servings are much too generous. Sometimes I wish I could ask the waiter to bring half a portion. Only for dessert are we allowed to show some restraint. Today, even in fancy restaurants, one can request two, four, or even six spoons with one chocolate cake without being frowned upon. A little taste for all satisfies our desire for chocolate without the calories!

The recipes in this book are not all mine. In some cases, they were originally given to me by relatives, friends, chefs, hosts, as well as by some of the wonderful cooks who have helped me entertain over the years. But I have tweaked them here and there to reflect my personal philosophy: Small changes make the biggest difference. A little less of this, a little less of that, and soon, you will discover, as I did, that there is much delight in eating right.

A HEALTHY KITCHEN

Variety is the spice of life.

Bringing color and creativity into the kitchen is the best way to ensure a diet that benefits your overall health, and it's the best way to give your body the nutrients it needs in the way it is naturally designed to use them.

Choosing high-quality ingredients that are as close to natural as possible is a good beginning. Buying organic, which refers to the way foods are produced and processed, is a commitment to agricultural practices that strive for a balance with nature, using methods and materials that are of low impact to the environment. The primary goal of farming organically is to optimize the health and productivity of interdependent communities of soil life, plants, animals, and people. Although slightly more expensive, organic meat, eggs, dairy, and produce are becoming widely available. It seems to make sense to purchase food that is as close to its natural state as possible, without the addition of growth hormones, antibiotics, dangerous pesticides, and chemicals. In addition, many people believe that organic foods taste better!

Healthful food is fresh, seasonal, and full of taste, texture, and essential nutrients.

Different types of fruits and vegetables are the cornerstones of a healthy diet and balance the other nutritional necessities: whole grains and legumes, fat-free or low-fat dairy foods, lean protein, and healthy oils from fish, nut, and vegetable sources.

Eating five to nine servings a day of fruits

BEHIND THE ORGANIC SEAL

The USDA approved four organic label categories, only two of which are permitted to display the USDA Organic seal.

100% Organic: 100% organically produced raw or processed foods where nothing has been added, including vitamins and minerals.

Organic: 95% organically produced raw or processed foods that contain 5% non-organic materials approved by the USDA and for which no organic option is available.

Made with Organic: At least 70% of content is organic, and the front product panel may display the phrase "Made with Organic" followed by up to three specific ingredients. (May not display the USDA Organic seal.)

Less Than 70% of Content Is Organic: May list only those ingredients that are organic on the ingredient panel with no mention of organic on the main panel. (May not display the USDA Organic seal.)

BLUE/PURPLE FOODS

Blackberries
Black currants
Blueberries
Blue potatoes
Dried plums (prunes)
Eggplant
Plums
Purple asparagus
Purple cabbage
Purple figs
Purple grapes
Purple peppers
Raisins

and vegetables, made up of a variety of different colors, promotes good health by providing the body with a palate of vitamins, minerals, and phytochemicals essential for maintaining health and fighting disease. These protective compounds work alone and in combination to nourish and protect the body. Often, the chemicals that are responsible for the colors of fruits and vegetables—for example, beets are red because of the phytochemical betacyanin—are the same ones that are good for us, so the lesson is to eat a rainbow of colors for health and well-being.

Purple and blue fruits and vegetables contain the health-promoting phytochemicals anthocyanins and phenolics, which are thought to be important for their antioxidant, anti-aging, cancer-preventing, and memory-preserving effects. It's easy to add these exotically colored foods to your diet. Mix a handful of blueberries into fat-free plain yogurt, snack on purple grapes after dinner, or make a salad from purple cabbage.

We all know to eat our greens, and there are many different kinds to enjoy. Green vegetables contain potent phytochemicals such as lutein and indoles, currently being studied for their potential antioxidant benefits. Remember, the darker the green, the more packed with nutrients that benefit bones, teeth, and vision.

Orange and yellow fruits and vegetables

GREEN FOODS

Artichokes
Arugula
Asparagus
Avocados
Broccoli
Brussels sprouts
Celery
Chinese cabbage
Cucumbers
Green apples
Green beans
Green cabbage
Green grapes
Green herbs
Green onions
Green pears
Green peppers
Green-fleshed melons
Kiwifruit
Leafy greens
Leeks
Lettuce
Limes
Okra
Peas
Snow peas
Spinach
Sugar snap peas
Watercress

Apricots
Butternut squash
Cantaloupe
Carrots
Golden kiwifruit
Grapefruit
Kumquats
Lemons
Mangoes
Nectarines
Oranges
Papayas
Peaches
Persimmons
Pineapples
Pumpkins
Sweet corn
Sweet potatoes
Tangerines
Yellow apples
Yellow figs
Yellow pears
Yellow peppers
Yellow potatoes
Yellow summer squash
Yellow tomatoes
Yellow winter squash

are an easy choice to include in meals all year around, as they are full of flavor and nutrients. They contain antioxidants such as vitamin C as well as carotenoids and bioflavonoids, two phytochemicals that are thought to lower the risk of some cancers and help maintain heart, vision, skin, and immune system health. My much-loved Carrot and Papaya Soup (page 77) features these wonderful ingredients, as does my Pureed Sweet Potatoes (page 157).

Red fruits and vegetables are as varied in their flavors—from the sweet of strawberries and cherries to the bitter of radicchio—as they are in their nutritive benefits, which range from helping to lower cancer risk to maintaining heart and urinary tract health and memory function. They contain the phytochemicals lycopene and anthocyanins and have some of the highest amounts of antioxidants.

Even though the emphasis is on color in our food, the white, tan, and brown fruits and vegetables still have many benefits, as they naturally come in those hues and have not been processed to end up this way. Think of sweet white corn that is a special treat of summer or banana pulp that is a great source of vital potassium. These fruits and vegetables help maintain cholesterol levels and heart health, and they also contain powerful phytochemicals,

HOW TO CHOOSE PRODUCE

Look at the produce you are buying. Make sure it has no blemishes, bruises, or punctures in the skin. As you shop, pick up the produce and smell it. Does it smell like a melon should, for instance? Don't be afraid to touch and test the produce. If a pineapple is ripe, you can easily pull a leaf from the center of the top. Smell the bottom. If it smells like sweet pineapple, it's ready to eat. For fruits like avocados and melons, lightly press where the stem was attached to see if it gives a little, a sure hint of ripeness. Water weighs a lot, so juicy fruits should feel heavy in your hand; this is the best way to judge that the fruit is not dry. If it's light, put it back.

If fruit is not as ripe as you need, here's a trick I use: Place it in a paper bag with an apple and set it on a windowsill that gets sun. Voilà! After a day or two, it will be ready to eat.

RED FOODS

Beets

Blood oranges

Cherries

Cranberries

Pink/red grapefruit

Pomegranates

Radicchio

Radishes

Raspberries

Red apples

Red grapes

Red onions

Red pears

Red peppers

Red potatoes

Rhubarb

Strawberries

Tomatoes

Watermelon

like allicin, which is found in the onion family.

In addition to nutrient-dense fruits and vegetables, whole grains—as well as legumes, nuts, and seeds—are vital to our diet and are the staple of many people around the world. In their whole state, these foods are predominantly brown. Unfortunately, our palates have become used to grains in their refined state, where the fiber-rich hull and nutrient-dense germ have been removed. By simply substituting brown for white, you can make a leap forward in improving the nutrient quality of your diet. Try grains such as barley, quinoa, and brown rice. Be adventurous and try the "forbidden" or black rice as a dessert. Also try legumes, including beans, peas, and lentils. Some of my favorites include Lentil Soup (page 75) and the chickpea-packed Lemon Hummus (page 104) served with fish or chicken. Seeds are plentiful and add interesting flavor, texture, and bursts of nutrients to meals. They are a good plant source of vital omega-3 fatty acids, so important to heart health and also wonderful for nourishing the skin.

So remember that the best way to get the nutrients your body needs is by eating foods as close as possible to their whole form and by choosing foods with a wide variety of colors and textures. Soon you will awaken your senses and palate to the nutrients provided by Mother Nature and reap the benefits.

WHITE FOODS

Bananas

Brown pears

Cauliflower

Dates

Garlic

Ginger

Jerusalem artichokes

Jícama

Mushrooms

Onions

Parsnips

Turnips

White nectarines

White peaches

White potatoes

KITCHEN EQUIPMENT

Here are the basic must-haves in every kitchen:

- A really good set of knives, which includes a paring knife, an all-purpose knife, a carving knife, a large knife for chopping that has a wide blade, and a bread knife. In addition, I like poultry shears for cutting chickens after they have been roasted or barbecued. Don't forget a sharpening steel: A good cook keeps his or her knives sharp, always.

- Two small cutting boards, about 8 by 10 inches (20 by 25 cm) each. I also like a large one for cutting meat.

- Various sizes of nonstick skillets; my favorite is made by Farberware and is called Millennium. What I like about it is that one can use metal forks and spoons, as well as plastic, for stirring, serving, and scooping things out, and the surface doesn't scratch.

- Various sizes of stainless steel (with copper inside for even distribution of heat) pots with lids: large ones for making broths and smaller ones for sauces, soups, and vegetables

- Nonstick crêpe pans with curved sides

- Juice extractor; my favorite is by Braun

- Blender

- Food processor

- Vegetable steamer or steamer basket

- Garlic press

- Melon scoop

- Cherry pitter

- Grapefruit knife

- Measuring cups and spoons

- Nut crackers

- Tongs

- Small and large strainers

- Colander

- Grater, either flat or standing, with different-size grating teeth

- Stainless steel ladles and spatulas

- Strawberry huller

- Whisks

- Large-handled parer

- Stainless steel bowl

- A set of mixing bowls made of glass or porcelain

- High-wattage microwave

- Citrus juicer

- Nonstick cookie sheet

- Nonstick rack for roasting poultry

- Roasting pan

- Coffeemaker that uses filter papers

- Wooden stirring spoons

- Ovenproof glass baking dishes

- Ovenproof round tart pans and pie plates

- Stainless steel tea kettle. I love the ones designed each year by Michael Graves for Target. They're fun and high quality—I must have five in my collection!

BILL LIEBERMAN'S YOGURT SHAKE

Noted for his youthful appearance, Bill Lieberman worked as a curator at the Metropolitan Museum of Art for many years. In his eighties, he was the most energetic, intelligent, and articulate individual I believe I had ever met. One day, seated at lunch between Bill and David Hockney, I asked him what he attributed his tremendous robust health to, and he gave me his secret recipe that I have enjoyed now for many years. Although I prefer my orange juice separately, for extra zing it is delicious in this drink.

SERVES 2

12	ounces (340 g) low-fat plain yogurt
1	ripe banana
½	cup (120 ml) carrot juice
¼	cup (60 ml) orange juice
8	strawberries

Place the yogurt, banana, carrot juice, orange juice, and strawberries in a blender or food processor and blend until smooth. Serve.

Per serving: 220 calories, 3 g total fat, 1.5 g saturated fat, 10 g protein, 41 g carbohydrates, 4 g dietary fiber, 130 mg sodium

LEFT TO RIGHT: MINT SMOOTHIE (PAGE 58), ALMOND MILK AND PEACH SMOOTHIE (PAGE 24), AND EVERY BERRY SMOOTHIE (PAGE 25)

ALMOND MILK AND PEACH SMOOTHIE

Almonds are high in protein and omega fatty acids and are cholesterol free. They are high in vitamin E, a powerful antioxidant, and contain minerals such as zinc, magnesium, potassium, calcium, and iron. In fact, 1 ounce (30 g) of almonds contains 10 percent of the recommended daily intake of calcium.

SERVES 2

3	ripe peaches, peeled and sliced, or 2 cups (455 g) frozen peaches
¾	cup (180 ml) almond milk
6	ounces (170 g) fat-free plain yogurt
2	tablespoons (30 ml) pure maple syrup
	Ice cubes, crushed
⅛	teaspoon ground star anise or nutmeg

Place the peaches in a blender or food processor and pulse to puree. Add the milk, yogurt, and maple syrup and continue to blend until smooth. Pour over crushed ice and sprinkle with the star anise or nutmeg just before serving.

Per serving: 190 calories, 1.5 g total fat, 0 g saturated fat, 8 g protein, 40 g carbohydrates, 3 g dietary fiber, 140 mg sodium

EVERY BERRY SMOOTHIE

Berries are bursting with healthy phytonutrients, such as anthocyanin pigments, powerful antioxidants responsible for the purplish black color of blackberries and blueberries. A cup of strawberries contains more than 100 milligrams of vitamin C, almost as much as a cup of orange juice.

SERVES 2

2 cups mixed fresh or frozen berries, such as blueberries, blackberries, raspberries, and strawberries

½ cup (120 ml) pear juice

½ ripe banana

1 cup (230 g) fat-free plain yogurt

Place the berries in a blender or food processor and blend, gradually adding the pear juice, until smooth. Add the banana and yogurt and continue to blend until smooth. Serve over ice, if desired.

Per serving: 180 calories, 1 g total fat, 0 g saturated fat, 7 g protein, 43 g carbohydrates, 7 g dietary fiber, 70 mg sodium

GOODNESS IN A GLASS

Homemade juices and smoothies are a quick, tasty way of meeting your daily fruit and vegetable quota. Yogurt is a useful foundation for delicious smoothies, and the good bacteria in yogurt are very beneficial for the bacteria balance in the digestive system.

An 8-ounce (240 ml) glass of freshly squeezed juice counts as one portion of the five servings of fruit and vegetables you should aim for. Make up the rest with salads, fresh and dried fruit, and raw or lightly cooked vegetables with your meals.

If you're buying a juicer, look for a continuous-feed type. It has one outlet delivering the juice and another sending out the pulp, which makes it the easiest kind to use. Failing that, choose one with a large waste capacity or you will be constantly stopping to empty it.

My advice to friends who've just had a face-lift is to drink a remedy of papaya and pineapple juices. The enzymes—papain in papayas and bromelain in pineapples—seem to work wonders to reduce swelling and bruising, and the mixture is delicious as well.

THE MOST DELICIOUS FRUIT SALAD, EVER

This fruit salad seems complicated, but I promise it truly lives up to its name and is worth the effort.

SERVES 6 TO 8

½	grapefruit
1	navel orange
1	cup seedless grapes
1	cup blueberries
1	cup blackberries
1	cup raspberries
1	cup strawberries
1	cup pitted cherries
½	Granny Smith or McIntosh apple, cut into ½-inch (1.3 cm) pieces
1	cantaloupe slice, about 1 inch (2.5 cm) thick, cut into ½-inch (1.3 cm) pieces
1	honeydew slice, about 1 inch (2.5 cm) thick, cut into ½-inch (1.3 cm) pieces
1	pineapple slice, about ½ inch (1.3 cm) thick, cut into ½-inch (1.3 cm) pieces
1	apricot, cut into 6 wedges, then cut in half
1	peach, cut into 8 wedges, then cut in half
1	nectarine, cut into 8 wedges, then cut in half
1	cup (240 ml) plus 2 tablespoons (30 ml) orange juice
	Juice of ½ lemon
¼	cup (60 g) apricot jam
1	banana, sliced
2	tablespoons (30 ml) rose water
2	tablespoons (30 ml) Cointreau, Triple Sec, or Grand Marnier (optional)

Using a very sharp knife, remove all the skin and pith from the grapefruit and orange. Slide the knife down one side of each fruit segment, then cut down the other side and gently pull out the segment. Place the berries in a colander and rinse, picking over to remove any soft berries or stems. Place the segments and berries in a large bowl with all the other fruit (except the banana). Add 1 cup (240 ml) of the orange juice and the lemon juice; gently toss to combine. Cover and refrigerate until ready to serve.

Just before serving, combine the jam and the remaining 2 tablespoons (30 ml) orange juice in a small saucepan. Stir over low heat until the jam is completely melted.

Remove the salad from the refrigerator; add the banana, warm jam mixture, rose water, and Cointreau, Triple Sec, or Grand Marnier, if using. Gently toss to combine and divide among individual bowls.

Per serving (based on 6 servings): 230 calories, 1 g total fat, 0 g saturated fat, 3 g protein, 62 g carbohydrates, 8 g dietary fiber, 15 mg sodium

EXERCISE, SUNSHINE, AND FRESH AIR

Healthy people are easy to recognize: They stand straight, their eyes sparkle, their skin glows, and they smile readily. Besides getting a diet of fresh food, it is equally important for us to move our bodies every day. Oxygen is the other vital ingredient that we cannot obtain from food. Our bodies carry about 1 quart of oxygen in the blood at any one time. Our hearts are responsible for pumping blood and oxygen to every blood cell and removing the carbon dioxide and other impurities from the body through our lungs and kidneys. Exercise is the best way to stimulate our bodies' ability to remove these waste products, strengthen our muscles, and calm our minds.

It has been recognized since ancient times that the "life force" and breath are interconnected. Along with the nutrients from our food, it is the breath that keeps us alive and sustains each of our bodies' systems in good health.

Exercise does not have to be an effort, and like eating healthy food, it is what you do most often that becomes a habit. When I'm at home, I have a trainer who works with me three times a week with weights and mat work to maintain strength and flexibility. But when schedules change, I fit in exercise that does not require me to change into workout clothes and go to the gym. I take the stairs whenever I can, around the house I make sure to walk at a good pace, and I run as many errands as time permits on foot—so wearing comfortable shoes is a must!

I love a game of singles tennis to keep my "blood boiling," and I fit this in once a week, as much for the body as the mind, and I swim whenever I get the chance. On vacations I take advantage of the open space and love to cross-country ski or hike. The key is to move every day to elevate the heart rate just enough to increase the flow of blood through the entire body and work the muscles while taking joy in each breath. My advice is to get some fresh air every day, for at least 20 minutes, and before long it will become as natural as eating right. These two habits will sustain a healthy body for life.

SUN-DRIED FRUIT COMPOTE WITH ALMOND BREAD

Sun-dried or natural fruit, as opposed to commonly available packaged dried fruit, has a much more intense flavor. Keep a variety of fruit in the pantry to snack on or to rehydrate for this compote recipe.

SERVES 4 TO 6

10	dried peach, nectarine, apricot, or pear halves
12	dried pitted prunes
6	dried figs, halved
1/2	cup dried cherries or strawberries
1/4	cup dried currants, raisins, or cranberries
1	tablespoon (15 ml) orange-flower water (optional)
1	teaspoon cardamom pods, cracked
1	strip orange zest
	Juice of 1/2 lemon
	Almond Bread (page 30)

Place the fruit in a large bowl, sprinkle with orange-flower water, if using, and add enough cold water to cover. Stir, cover, and let stand overnight.

Transfer to a saucepan and add more water just to cover. Tie the cardamom pods and orange zest in a piece of cheesecloth or muslin. Add to the pan, bring to a boil, and simmer for 10 minutes. Allow to cool, remove the cardamom packet, and stir in the lemon juice. Serve warm or cold with almond bread.

Per serving (based on 4 servings without bread): 290 calories, 0.5 g total fat, 0 g saturated fat, 3 g protein, 74 g carbohydrates, 12 g dietary fiber, 5 mg sodium

ALMOND BREAD

This easy loaf is also great toasted and served with sliced banana drizzled with lemon and a generous dollop of low-fat yogurt.

MAKES 1 LOAF / 12 SLICES

4	tablespoons (60 g) butter, melted, plus extra for the loaf pan
1	cup whole-wheat flour
1	cup unbleached all-purpose flour
¾	cup almond meal
½	cup packed brown sugar
2½	teaspoons baking powder
1	teaspoon ground cinnamon
½	teaspoon salt
2	large eggs
1	cup (240 ml) low-fat milk

Per slice: 200 calories, 9 g total fat, 3 g saturated fat, 5 g protein, 27 g carbohydrates, 2 g dietary fiber, 250 mg sodium

Preheat the oven to 350°F (180°C). Butter a 9-inch (22 cm) loaf pan.

In a large bowl, mix the flours, almond meal, brown sugar, baking powder, cinnamon, and salt. In another bowl, beat together the eggs, milk, and 4 tablespoons (60 g) melted butter. Pour into the dry ingredients and mix well.

Pour the batter into the loaf pan and bake for 1 hour, or until a skewer comes out clean when tested at the center of the loaf. Cool on a wire rack for 10 minutes before removing from the pan. Slice to serve.

FREEZING BREAD

My son Gary taught me a technique for freezing bread and bagels that keeps them free of freezer burn. You can store bread twice as long as usual by using this method.

Snugly wrap the pieces with plastic wrap, being certain not to leave any air bubbles. Then wrap again with heavy-duty aluminum foil. Label the contents, including the date.

Before warming the frozen bread in the oven, be sure to remove the plastic wrap.

SAUTÉED RIPE PLANTAINS

Plantains, sometimes called "potatoes of the air," are extremely popular in Latin American countries as well as parts of Africa, Asia, and India. They are close relatives of bananas and are typically eaten cooked instead of raw. Plantains are high in potassium, which is needed to regulate water balance, blood pressure, and neuromuscular function.

I serve these plantains sprinkled with sugar at breakfast or as a quick carbohydrate dish with chicken or fish. Be sure to choose plantains that are very ripe—the peel should be half black. The pulp should be firm and smell sweet.

SERVES 4

2	very ripe plantains
1	tablespoon (15 ml) canola oil
1	tablespoon brown sugar (optional)
¼	cup (60 g) fat-free sour cream (optional)

Per serving: 90 calories, 3.5 g total fat, 0 g saturated fat, 1 g protein, 16 g carbohydrates, 2 g dietary fiber, 0 mg sodium

Peel the plantains and slice on the diagonal. Heat the oil in a large nonstick skillet over medium heat. Add the slices in a single layer and cook until browned and crispy on both sides, about 10 minutes. Serve immediately. If desired, sprinkle with the brown sugar and serve with the sour cream.

TOASTED GRAIN AND NUT SUNDAES WITH BERRIES

Berries are the stars of summer—at their peak in June and July and bursting with flavor. This is a breakfast version of a make-your-own sundae, and you can vary the layers according to your taste.

SERVES 4

1	cup quick-cooking rolled oats
1/3	cup sliced almonds
1/3	cup coarsely chopped walnuts
1 1/2	tablespoons (23 ml) walnut oil or extra-virgin olive oil
2	tablespoons (30 ml) honey
10	strawberries, quartered
1	cup mixed berries, such as blueberries, blackberries, and raspberries
	Juice of 1 lemon
2	cups (450 g) fat-free plain yogurt

Per serving: 360 calories, 17 g total fat, 1.5 g saturated fat, 12 g protein, 45 g carbohydrates, 6 g dietary fiber, 70 mg sodium

Preheat the oven to 350°F (180°C). In a medium bowl, mix the oats, almonds, walnuts, oil, and honey.

Spread the mixture on a rimmed baking sheet and bake, stirring occasionally with a wooden spoon, for 20 minutes, or until the mixture turns golden brown. Set aside to cool.

Combine the berries in a bowl. Transfer half of the berries and the lemon juice to a small saucepan and cook over low heat for 5 minutes, pressing down on the berries as they cook to extract the juice. Return the cooked berries to the others and stir to combine.

In 4 sundae glasses, layer the fruit, yogurt, and oat mixture until the glasses are filled. Top with berries and serve with long spoons.

VANILLA-SCENTED GRANOLA

This is a healthy granola that provides a wide variety of nutrients and fiber without the fat and sugar content of many store-bought granolas. Served with some poached fruit or fresh berries and some yogurt, it would be a delight on a brunch buffet. The granola can be made 2 weeks ahead and stored in an airtight container at room temperature.

SERVES 12

1	cup rolled barley flakes
2	cups old-fashioned rolled oats
½	cup almonds, roughly chopped
½	cup hazelnuts, roughly chopped
¼	cup sunflower seeds
¼	cup pumpkin seeds
¼	cup sesame seeds
¼	cup wheat germ
¼	cup ground flaxseed
¼	cup (60 ml) walnut oil
¼	cup (60 ml) honey
¼	cup (60 ml) molasses
¼	cup (60 ml) vanilla extract
1	cup raisins or dried cherries

Per serving: 350 calories, 17 g total fat, 1.5 g saturated fat, 9 g protein, 41 g carbohydrates, 5 g dietary fiber, 10 mg sodium

Preheat the oven to 300°F (150°C). Line a rimmed baking sheet with parchment paper.

In large bowl, mix the barley, oats, almonds, hazelnuts, sunflower seeds, pumpkin seeds, sesame seeds, wheat germ, and flaxseed.

In a small saucepan, combine the oil, honey, and molasses and bring to a simmer over medium heat. Remove from the heat and stir in the vanilla extract. Pour over the oat mixture and stir well.

Spread the granola evenly on the baking sheet. Bake, stirring occasionally, for 30 minutes, or until golden brown (check after 20 minutes).

Cool on a wire rack and stir in the raisins or dried cherries.

SWISS MUESLI

This is similar to Swedish Bircher muesli but without the cream. It is a very popular way to begin the day in Switzerland, and it is one way I start my day. You can make this using either fat-free milk or apple juice, depending on the texture that appeals to you. I use Familia Swiss Muesli with no added sugar, but any unsweetened raw muesli will be delicious. To make an attractive presentation, I often serve it in a martini glass.

SERVES 4

2	cups unsweetened raw muesli
4	cups (1 liter) fat-free milk or unsweetened apple juice
2	apples, grated
1	cup berries
2	small bananas, sliced
1	cup (230 g) fat-free plain yogurt
	Ground cinnamon (optional)

Combine the muesli with the milk in a bowl, cover, and refrigerate overnight. In the morning, spoon into serving bowls and top with the apple, berries, and banana slices. Serve with the yogurt and sprinkle with the cinnamon, if desired.

Per serving: 390 calories, 2.5 g total fat, 0 g saturated fat, 16 g protein, 81 g carbohydrates, 7 g dietary fiber, 210 mg sodium

BREAKFAST IN A MUFFIN

Full of good nutrients to start the day, these easy muffins can be made ahead so you can pick one up on your way out the door. Adding fruit to these muffins is a great way to help make up the minimum of five servings of fruit and vegetables we need each day.

MAKES 12

1	cup whole-wheat flour
½	cup unbleached all-purpose flour
2	teaspoons baking powder
¼	teaspoon ground cinnamon
	Pinch of salt
¾	cup raisins, chopped prunes, or dried cherries or strawberries
2	tablespoons wheat germ
1	cup (230 g) fat-free plain yogurt
½	cup (120 ml) honey
2	tablespoons (30 ml) extra-virgin olive oil
1	large egg
	Grated zest of ½ orange
2	tablespoons (30 ml) orange juice
1	cup berries or chopped fruit, such as pears or peaches (optional)

Per muffin: 170 calories, 3 g total fat, 0 g saturated fat, 4 g protein, 33 g carbohydrates, 2 g dietary fiber, 125 mg sodium

Preheat the oven to 400°F (200°C). Line 12 muffin cups with paper liners or grease with olive oil.

Sift the flours, baking powder, cinnamon, and salt into a large bowl. Stir in the raisins and wheat germ. Make a well in the center of the dry ingredients.

In a medium bowl, mix the yogurt, honey, oil, egg, orange zest, and orange juice. Pour into the dry ingredients and stir until just combined. Stir in the berries or chopped fruit, if using. Spoon the mixture into the muffin cups.

Bake for 20 to 28 minutes (longer with the addition of the fruit), until the muffins are golden brown and the centers are firm when gently touched; rotate the pan after about 10 minutes. Cool in the pan for 2 to 3 minutes before turning out onto a wire rack to cool completely.

FRENCH TOAST

In my opinion, French toast is the best way to use up day-old bread, and for special occasions the traditional bread called challah is a delicious treat. But you can view this recipe as a way to experiment with all sorts of delicious breads, from whole grain to raisin cinnamon, to vary the texture and flavor.

SERVES 6 TO 8

6	large eggs
½	cup (120 ml) milk
½	teaspoon (2 ml) vanilla extract
½	teaspoon (2 ml) almond extract
½	teaspoon (2 ml) orange extract
½	teaspoon (2 ml) lemon extract
1	tablespoon superfine (caster) sugar
	Pinch of salt
8	slices day-old or stale country loaf, whole-grain bread, or challah
	Canola oil
	Pure maple syrup, warmed
	Berries and banana for serving (optional)

In a medium bowl, whisk together the eggs, milk, extracts, sugar, and salt. Pour into a large baking dish and lay the bread slices in the mixture. Wait for 5 minutes before turning to coat both sides. Cover and refrigerate for at least 1 hour or overnight.

Preheat the oven to 250°F (120°C).

Lightly grease a large nonstick skillet with oil and place over medium heat for 1 minute. Place 2 slices of bread at a time into the skillet and cook for 2 to 3 minutes per side, until golden brown. Transfer to a plate and keep warm in the oven while the rest of the French toast is prepared. Serve with warm maple syrup, berries, and sliced banana, if desired.

Per serving (based on 6 servings): 310 calories, 10 g total fat, 2.5 g saturated fat, 11 g protein, 44 g carbohydrates, 3 g dietary fiber, 300 mg sodium

HONEY-SPELT SCONES

A wonderfully nutritious and ancient grain with a deep
nutlike flavor, spelt is a cousin to wheat but offers a broader
spectrum of plant nutrients. Served with fresh ricotta
cheese and jam or fruit spread, these scones are delicious
any time of the day.

MAKES 6

1¼	cups spelt flour, plus extra for the counter and baking sheet
1	tablespoon baking powder
½	teaspoon baking soda
¼	teaspoon salt
½	cup (120 ml) water
3	tablespoons (45 ml) honey
1	tablespoon (15 ml) extra-virgin olive oil, plus extra for the baking sheet

Per scone: 140 calories, 3.5 g total fat, 0 g saturated
fat, 3 g protein, 27 g carbohydrates, 2 g dietary fiber,
450 mg sodium

Preheat the oven to 375°F (190°C). Grease and
flour a baking sheet.

In a large bowl, mix the flour, baking powder,
baking soda, and salt. Add the water, honey, and
oil and mix vigorously. Allow the dough to rest
for 15 minutes.

Turn the dough out onto a floured counter and
flatten with your hands to 1 inch (2.5 cm) thick.
Use biscuit cutters or the top end of a glass to
cut out rounds of dough and place on the baking
sheet.

Bake for 10 to 12 minutes, until golden. Cool on a
wire rack.

BUCKWHEAT WAFFLES

Buckwheat is a fruit seed that is related to rhubarb and sorrel, making it a suitable grain substitute for people with gluten sensitivity. Serve these waffles with sliced fresh strawberries and maple syrup for a scrumptious breakfast.

MAKES 6 TO 8

1½	cups buckwheat flour or chestnut flour
1½	cups unbleached all-purpose flour
¼	cup superfine (caster) sugar
4	teaspoons baking powder
1½	teaspoons baking soda
½	teaspoon salt
6	large eggs
3	cups (720 ml) low-fat buttermilk
6	tablespoons (90 g) butter, melted and cooled

Heat a waffle iron according to the manufacturer's directions. In a large bowl, mix the flours, sugar, baking powder, baking soda, and salt.

In another large bowl, beat the eggs with a hand-held electric mixer until fluffy. Beat in the buttermilk and butter. Add to the dry ingredients and mix until just blended. Transfer the batter to a pitcher.

Pour the batter onto the center of the hot waffle iron. Bake about 5 minutes, or until the steaming stops. Remove carefully and repeat with the remaining batter.

Per serving (based on 6 servings): 440 calories, 17 g total fat, 9 g saturated fat, 18 g protein, 53 g carbohydrates, 5 g dietary fiber, 1,120 mg sodium

BUCKWHEAT

Buckwheat has a robust, nutlike flavor and is perhaps the most distinctive of any food eaten as a grain. The particularly assertive taste of roasted buckwheat marries well with other hearty-flavored, densely textured foods, such as beef, root vegetables, cabbage, winter squash, roasted peppers, and eggplant. Nutritionally, the protein in buckwheat is of high quality because it contains all eight essential amino acids in good proportions.

PLAIN PANCAKES

Pancake batter can be made ahead of time and left to rest for 2 hours. Whether drizzled with maple syrup or simply squeezed with fresh lemon juice and a sprinkle of sugar, fresh pancakes are undeniably a treat.

MAKES 6 TO 8 PANCAKES OR 36 SILVER DOLLAR PANCAKES

1   cup unbleached all-purpose flour
    Pinch of salt
2   large eggs, lightly beaten
1   cup (240 ml) fat-free milk
1   teaspoon (5 ml) canola oil, plus extra
    for the skillet

Per 6 silver dollar pancakes or 1 regular pancake: 130 calories, 3.5 g total fat, 0.5 g saturated fat, 6 g protein, 18 g carbohydrates, 0 g dietary fiber, 90 mg sodium

Preheat the oven to 250°F (120°C).

Sift the flour and salt into a medium bowl and make a well in the center. In a separate bowl, mix the eggs, milk, and 1 teaspon (5 ml) oil. Pour into the dry ingredients and mix until a smooth batter forms. Transfer to a pitcher or large measuring cup.

Lightly grease a large nonstick skillet with oil and place over medium heat for 1 minute. Pour enough batter into the pan to make pancakes 3 to 4 inches (7.5 to 10 cm) in diameter (for silver dollars, use 1 tablespoon [15 ml] batter). Cook until bubbles appear on the surface and the underside is golden, about 1 minute for larger pancakes. Using a spatula, flip the pancakes and cook for another 45 to 60 seconds before turning out onto a warm plate. Keep the cooked pancakes warm in the oven while preparing the rest of the pancakes.

MY SECRET RECIPE FOR PANCAKES

The "secret" ingredient here and in my crêpes is simply the addition of the citrus, vanilla, and almond extracts. They bring plain pancakes up to a new level.

SERVES 6 TO 8

3	recipes Plain Pancakes (page 39)
2	tablespoons superfine (caster) sugar
1/2	teaspoon (2 ml) vanilla extract
1/2	teaspoon (2 ml) almond extract
1/2	teaspoon (2 ml) orange extract
1/2	teaspoon (2 ml) lemon extract

Per serving (based on 6 servings): 400 calories, 10 g total fat, 2 g saturated fat, 17 g protein, 58 g carbohydrates, 2 g dietary fiber, 270 mg sodium

In a very large bowl, combine the pancake batter, sugar, and extracts. Cook as for regular or silver dollar pancakes.

VARIATION

For Blueberry Pancakes: Add 4 to 6 blueberries to each tablespoon (15 ml) of batter just before flipping the pancakes.

NOTES ABOUT PANCAKE BATTER AND CRÊPES

My mother was born in Vienna, and she was a very good cook. She taught me a simple and easy way of making pancakes and crêpes, so they will be perfect each time. When you beat the batter and lift the whisk from the bowl, there will be a stream that runs from the end of the whisk back into the bowl. Your preference for thin or thick pancakes will decide the thickness of the stream.

My family prefers our pancakes thin, so I check the consistency by holding the whisk up off the bowl at least 12 inches (30 cm). The stream will be thick for a thicker pancake and thin as you gradually add more milk to the mixture. For crêpes, the mixture needs to be a thin, continuous stream but not too thin—if the stream breaks, the crêpes will not hold together.

To test if the pan is hot enough for the batter, drop 1/4 teaspoon (2 ml) of batter onto the skillet. It will sizzle and bubble if the pan is ready. Make sure you remove the test pieces before pouring in the batter.

BUCKWHEAT SILVER DOLLAR PANCAKES

My grandson, Joshua, loves my Silver Dollar Pancakes. I think it was when he was about 7 or 8 years old, I asked him, "How many pancakes did you end up eating?" And he looked me straight in the face and said, "About 35," which knocked me off my chair.

MAKES 36

1	cup buckwheat flour
2	teaspoons baking powder
1	teaspoon baking soda
	Pinch of salt
2	large eggs, lightly beaten
1⅓	cups (320 ml) fat-free milk
	Melted butter

Preheat the oven to 250°F (120°C).

Sift the flour, baking powder, baking soda, and salt into a bowl and make a well in the center. In a separate bowl, mix the eggs and milk. Pour into the dry ingredients and mix until a smooth batter forms.

Brush a small nonstick skillet with butter and place over medium heat for 1 minute. For each pancake, spoon 1 tablespoon (15 ml) batter into the pan and cook until bubbles start to appear on the surface and the underside is golden, about 1 minute. Using a spatula, flip the pancakes and cook for 30 seconds more.

Keep the cooked pancakes warm in the oven while preparing the rest of the pancakes.

Per 6 silver dollar pancakes: 120 calories, 4 g total fat, 1.5 g saturated fat, 6 g protein, 13 g carbohydrates, 3 g dietary fiber, 480 mg sodium

APPLE SAUCE

This is a recipe that I originally learned as a child in cooking class. I've modified it to keep the skin on—the peel is full of pectin, which is water-soluble dietary fiber that can help lower blood cholesterol levels. Other dietary sources of soluble fiber include oat bran, barley, and legumes. Serve this sauce with pancakes or with corn fritters and roast chicken. I allow for one apple per person.

SERVES 4

4	large apples, preferably McIntosh or Rome, cored and sliced
1	tablespoon sugar
¼	teaspoon ground nutmeg
¼	teaspoon ground cloves
¼	teaspoon ground cinnamon (optional)
	Squeeze of fresh lemon juice

Per serving: 120 calories, 0 g total fat, 0 g saturated fat, 1 g protein, 33 g carbohydrates, 5 g dietary fiber, 0 mg sodium

Place the apples in a microwave-safe bowl and add a few drops of water. Cover and microwave on high for 8 to 10 minutes, or until soft; stir occasionally. Transfer to a food processor and process until very smooth. Add the sugar and season with the spices and lemon juice. Serve warm or chilled.

VARIATION

To make apple sauce on the stove top: Place the sliced apples in a heavy-based saucepan, add ½ cup (125 ml) water, and bring to a simmer over high heat. Cover and reduce the heat to medium. Cook until the apples are soft, about 10 to 12 minutes, stirring occasionally. Transfer to a food processor and continue as directed above.

MY SPECIAL CRÊPE RECIPE

These crêpes may be filled with either sweet fillings, such as pure fruit jam, or orange marmalade, and sprinkled with a little powdered sugar. They are also delicious with savory fillings and wonderful served with shredded vegetables as an appetizer. Children enjoy them with ham and low-fat cream cheese, and a popular sweet filling in France is Nutella. Use your imagination and a few of your preferred ingredients to develop your own favorites. We often make crêpes, so I have a nonstick crêpe (8-inch/20 cm) pan for each burner on my stove. It makes it easy to serve many people simultaneously.

SERVES 4

½   cup unbleached all-purpose flour
     Pinch of salt
1   large egg, lightly beaten
½   cup (120 ml) plus 4 tablespoons (60 ml) fat-free milk
1   teaspoon (5 ml) canola oil
     Dash of vanilla extract
     Dash of almond extract
     Dash of orange extract
     Dash of lemon extract
     Melted butter

Per serving: 110 calories, 3.5 g total fat, 1 g saturated fat, 5 g protein, 15 g carbohydrates, 0 g dietary fiber, 80 mg sodium

Sift the flour and salt into a medium bowl and make a well in the center. In a separate bowl, mix the egg, ½ cup (120 ml) of the milk, and oil. Pour into the dry ingredients and mix until a smooth batter forms. Add the vanilla, almond, orange, and lemon extracts and stir to combine.

While whisking the batter, gradually add the remaining 4 tablespoons (60 ml) milk. To check the stream of the mix, hold the whisk 12 inches (30 cm) above the bowl; aim for a thin stream that does not break.

Heat an 8-inch (20 cm) crêpe pan or skillet over medium-high heat. Sprinkle a few drops of water into the pan; if they sizzle, the pan is ready to use. Brush with a little melted butter.

Using a ¼-cup (60 ml) measure, pour the batter into the skillet. Immediately pick up the pan and tilt and swirl it so that the batter covers the entire bottom of the pan. Pour any excess batter back into the bowl.

Cook for 1 minute. Loosen the edges of the crêpe with a spatula. You can use a spatula to turn the crêpe, but I usually turn it with my fingers. Using both hands, I pick up the loosened edges with my thumb and index finger and quickly flip it over.

Cook on the other side until lightly golden (usually less than a minute) and slide it out onto a plate. Cover with waxed paper. Repeat with the remaining batter.

COTTAGE CHEESE CRÊPES

Here is a wonderful crêpe recipe that I have used for brunch for Leonard and myself. I love cherries, and I always take advantage of them in season, but when they are unavailable, you can substitute raspberries, strawberries, blueberries, or blackberries in this recipe.

SERVES 2

4	crêpes (page 44)
6	tablespoons (90 g) fat-free cottage cheese
$\frac{1}{2}$	teaspoon plus $\frac{1}{8}$ teaspoon superfine (caster) sugar
3	tablespoons (45 g) fat-free sour cream
$\frac{1}{8}$	teaspoon (0.5 ml) vanilla extract
12	cherries, pitted, juices reserved

Per serving: 320 calories, 7 g total fat, 2 g saturated fat, 19 g protein, 44 g carbohydrates, 1 g dietary fiber, 180 mg sodium

Prepare the crêpes and set aside.

In a small bowl, mix the cottage cheese and $\frac{1}{2}$ teaspoon of the sugar. Place one-quarter of the mixture in the center of each crêpe. Fold the ends of each crêpe in and over the cheese mixture. Place 2 crêpes on each warm serving plate.

In a small bowl, mix the sour cream, vanilla extract, and the remaining $\frac{1}{8}$ teaspoon sugar. Spoon over the crêpes and top with the cherries. Serve.

EGG WHITE OMELET WITH FRESH HERBS AND GOAT CHEESE

Egg white recipes are popular because they are a good way to get the beneficial protein in eggs without the fat contained in the yolk. This omelet makes a light start to the day and would be delicious served with toasted Irish soda bread or another tasty whole-grain bread.

SERVES 2

4	large egg whites
1	tablespoon (15 ml) water
3	tablespoons minced fresh herbs, such as lemon thyme, chives, chervil, flat-leaf parsley, and tarragon
1	teaspoon (5 ml) extra-virgin olive oil
2	tablespoons (30 g) crumbled goat cheese

Per serving: 100 calories, 6 g total fat, 2.5 g saturated fat, 10 g protein, 1 g carbohydrates, 0 g dietary fiber, 140 mg sodium

Whisk the egg whites and water in a medium bowl until light and fluffy. Stir in the herbs.

Brush a medium omelet pan with the oil and warm over medium heat. Add the egg mixture. Allow the egg whites to set and color slightly, 4 to 5 minutes, then add the cheese in a line down the center of the eggs. Fold opposite sides of the omelet into the center to overlap and turn out onto a warmed plate.

EGGS

Is that egg in your fridge still fresh? There's an easy way to tell. Place the egg in a bowl of water deep enough to cover it by a few inches. If the egg sinks to the bottom, it's fresh. If it rises to the top, discard it.

Eggs can be purchased in sizes ranging from small to jumbo. The most important thing to remember is that if a recipe doesn't specify a size, it's understood that you use a large egg.

To separate an egg, have two bowls in front of you. Begin by cracking the egg on the side of one bowl or on the counter. Working over the bowl, pour the yolk from one half of the shell to the other several times to separate it from the white. Then place the yolk in the second bowl.

If you find any yolk in the egg white, dampen the end of a kitchen towel and use the point of the towel to reach into the bowl to remove it—it will adhere to the dampness of the towel. It's better to break eggs when they are cold, but use them once they come to room temperature.

SPANISH OMELET
À LA LAUDER

Egg protein is the standard against which other food proteins are measured. Eggs are good sources of vitamins A, B_1, B_{12}, D, and E as well as folate, phosphorus, zinc, and iron. Eggs are one of the rare natural sources of vitamin D. I add water to make the eggs in this omelet light and fluffy, and I often serve this with tomato sauce.

SERVES 4

6   large eggs

3   tablespoons (45 ml) water

1   teaspoon (5 ml) light olive oil or canola oil

1   medium onion, peeled and finely chopped

1   tomato, diced

1   teaspoon minced fresh dill

     Pinch of ground cumin

     Freshly ground black pepper

Per serving: 130 calories, 8 g total fat, 2.5 g saturated fat, 10 g protein, 6 g carbohydrates, 0 g dietary fiber, 100 mg sodium

In a medium bowl, whisk the eggs with the water until fluffy.

Heat the oil in a nonstick omelet pan over medium-low heat and sauté the onion until transparent, about 2 minutes. Stir in the tomato, dill, and cumin; season with the pepper. Remove the tomato mixture from the pan and set aside. Wipe the pan to remove any vegetable residue. Lightly oil the pan and add the eggs, stirring gently 2 or 3 times, then leave to set. Cover the pan and cook until the underside is firm and light brown (the top might still be a bit runny). When the top is almost firm, add the tomato mixture back in. Fold the top over, roll onto a plate, and serve.

OMELETS

When removing an omelet from the pan, hold the handle from below using a pot holder. Tilt the pan toward the plate and the omelet will roll over more easily.

POACHED EGGS WITH BALSAMIC MUSHROOMS AND SPINACH

Mushrooms are rich in B vitamins and health-promoting minerals. This combination of mushrooms and spinach is a good way to get your vegetables in early in the day.

SERVES 4

SPINACH

1	teaspoon (5 ml) extra-virgin olive oil
2	garlic cloves, peeled and finely chopped
8	cups baby spinach leaves
	Kosher salt

MUSHROOMS

4	cups (1 liter) low-sodium chicken broth
8	small portobello mushrooms, stems trimmed
4	tablespoons balsamic vinegar

EGGS

1	tablespoon (15 ml) white wine vinegar
4	large eggs
	Chopped fresh flat-leaf parsley leaves
	Kosher salt and freshly ground black pepper

Per serving: 170 calories, 7 g total fat, 2 g saturated fat, 13 g protein, 17 g carbohydrates, 3 g dietary fiber, 250 mg sodium

For the spinach: Heat the oil and garlic in a large saucepan over low heat for 2 minutes, or until the garlic is fragrant. Add the spinach, cover, and cook for 2 minutes, or until wilted. Season with the salt. Turn off the heat and allow to stand until the eggs are ready.

For the mushrooms: Bring the broth to a boil in a medium saucepan over medium heat. Add the mushrooms, reduce the heat to low, and simmer while the eggs poach.

For the eggs: Fill a large skillet with water, add the white wine vinegar, and bring to a rolling boil over medium-high heat. Carefully break 1 egg into a custard cup and slide it into the boiling water; repeat (2 or 3 eggs can be cooked at a time if the pan is large enough). Reduce the heat to medium-low and simmer, basting the eggs with water, until the whites are just firm and the yolks still soft, 2 to 3 minutes. Before removing the eggs from the pan, add 2 mushrooms and some of the hot broth to each soup plate. Top each plate with 1 egg, removed with a slotted spoon. Sprinkle with the parsley. Season with salt and pepper and serve with the spinach on the side. Drizzle the mushrooms with the balsamic vinegar.

"OVER THE TOP" SCRAMBLED EGGS

If you want an elegant but easy brunch or breakfast dish, these scrambled eggs are the answer. Serve them in the shell and top with either caviar or thin strips of Nova Scotia salmon, and a dollop of crème fraîche or fat-free sour cream. Sometimes I even serve them as a first course for dinner.

SERVES 4

4	large eggs
4	teaspoons (20 ml) water
½	teaspoon (2 ml) extra-virgin olive oil
½	teaspoon (2.5 g) butter
	Caviar or thinly cut strips of Nova Scotia salmon (optional)
	Crème Fraîche (page 52) or fat-free sour cream (optional)
	Toast points, for serving

Per serving (without toast points): 80 calories, 6 g total fat, 2 g saturated fat, 6 g protein, 0 g carbohydrates, 0 g dietary fiber, 75 mg sodium

Using a very sharp knife, cut off the narrow end of each egg about 1 inch (2.5 cm) into the shell. Pour the eggs into a small bowl, rinse the shells, and set aside.

Gently whisk the eggs with the water until well combined. Warm the oil in a large nonstick skillet over low heat for 1 minute. Pour in the eggs and stir slowly with a wooden spoon until the eggs thicken and begin to scramble. Remove from the heat and use a small spoon to fill the empty shells mounded to the top.

If desired, garnish with the caviar or smoked salmon and a dollop of crème fraîche or sour cream. Serve with toast points.

CRÈME FRAÎCHE

This indulgently rich recipe is from my friend Barbara Tober, the retired editor-in-chief of *Brides* magazine and a great cook in her own right. It is a must for my scrambled egg dish or for those special occasions when a piece of apple pie needs some topping.

MAKES 1 CUP (240 ML)

1 cup (240 ml) heavy cream

2 tablespoons (30 ml) low-fat butter-milk

Per tablespoon: 50 calories, 6 g total fat, 3.5 g saturated fat, 0 g protein, 1 g carbohydrates, 0 g dietary fiber, 10 mg sodium

Pour the cream into a bowl and stir in the butter-milk. Cover with plastic wrap and leave in a warm place in the kitchen, such as on top of the refrigerator, for at least 24 hours. This will make a thin crème fraîche, which you can cover and refrigerate at this point.

To achieve a thicker consistency, which I prefer, stir and leave again, covered, for 12 to 24 hours. In the morning, stir again and refrigerate for up to 1 week.

TURKEY AND SWEET POTATO HASH

Sweet potatoes are a nice departure from the white potatoes traditionally used to make hash. It would be delicious served with Cranberry Relish (page 194) for a casual weekend breakfast.

SERVES 4

2   medium sweet potatoes, peeled and cut into $\frac{1}{2}$-inch (1.3 cm) square dice

Pinch of kosher salt, plus extra for seasoning

1   Granny Smith apple, cut into $\frac{1}{2}$-inch (1.3 cm) square dice

6   ounces (170 g) fat-free plain yogurt

Juice of $\frac{1}{2}$ lemon

1   tablespoon (15 ml) extra-virgin olive oil

1   medium red onion, peeled and chopped

3   cups (1 pound/450 g) cubed cooked turkey or chicken

1   tablespoon chopped fresh thyme

1   tablespoon chopped fresh rosemary leaves

Freshly ground black pepper

Per serving: 310 calories, 7 g total fat, 1.5 g saturated fat, 35 g protein, 27 g carbohydrates, 3 g dietary fiber, 180 mg sodium

Place the sweet potatoes and a pinch of salt in a medium saucepan. Cover with water and bring to a boil over high heat. Reduce the heat to medium and cook for 4 minutes. Add the apple and cook for another 2 minutes, until tender. Drain.

Transfer 1 cup of the mixture to a large bowl and mash using a fork. Stir in the yogurt and lemon juice. Add the remaining sweet potato mixture and stir gently to combine.

Heat the oil in a large nonstick skillet over medium heat. Add the onion and cook, stirring, for 2 minutes, or until softened. Add the turkey, thyme, and rosemary and cook, stirring occasionally, for 3 minutes, or until heated through.

Spoon the sweet potato mixture into the skillet and stir to combine. Season with salt and pepper. Press on the hash with a wide metal spatula and cook until the underside is golden, about 3 minutes. Cut the hash into servings, turn the pieces, and cook until golden, about 2 minutes longer. Serve immediately.

GRAVLAX

Lax means "salmon," and *gravning* is an ancient method of preservation that resembles marinating. Serve it with pumpernickel bread and honey mustard with chopped fresh dill, or a salad that includes arugula, sliced potatoes, and tomatoes, along with a fine chilled vodka or aquavit.

SERVES 6 TO 8

1	wild salmon, 4–6 pounds (2–3 kg), head and tail removed, cut into 2 whole fillets
¾	cup kosher salt
¾	cup sugar
2	teaspoons freshly ground black pepper
1	teaspoon ground allspice
1	teaspoon ground cardamom
¼	teaspoon ground cloves
¼	teaspoon finely ground fennel seeds
4	bunches fresh dill, roughly chopped, reserving ¼ cup for garnish

Per serving (based on 8 servings): 400 calories, 14 g total fat, 2 g saturated fat, 45 g protein, 19 g carbohydrates, 0 g dietary fiber, 4,330 mg sodium

Remove any small bones from the fish, using a strawberry huller or tweezers. Place the fillets on a board covered in parchment paper. Mix the salt, sugar, pepper, allspice, cardamom, cloves, and fennel in a small bowl. Rub the mixture into the fillets on all sides.

Spread one-third of the dill in a large shallow dish big enough to hold a fillet. Top with one fillet, skin side down and tail end facing to the right. Spread half of the remaining dill over the fish. Add the second fillet, skin side up and tail end facing to the left. Cover with the remaining dill.

Cover loosely with plastic wrap. Place a large cutting board on top of the fish and weigh down lightly using a large can. Refrigerate for 36 to 48 hours, turning the fillets every morning and night and pouring off any accumulated liquid.

The fish is ready to eat. Scrape off the spices and dill, slice off the skin, and cut thin slices on the diagonal on the broad surface of the fillet (like shavings). Garnish with the reserved ¼ cup dill. Gravlax keeps for about a week in the refrigerator.

NOON

MINT SMOOTHIE

Buttermilk is made by adding cultured bacteria to pasteurized fat-free or low-fat milk, just like yogurt. Combined with the mint, which is known to aid digestion, this stimulating smoothie is a nice accompaniment to a light salad at lunch.

SERVES 2

1½	cups (360 ml) low-fat buttermilk
¼	cup (60 ml) water
2	cups fresh mint leaves
½	teaspoon ground cumin
1	cup ice cubes
2	fresh mint sprigs

Place the buttermilk, water, mint leaves, and cumin in a blender or food processor and blend until smooth. Add the ice and continue to blend another 30 seconds. Pour into glasses and garnish with the mint sprigs just before serving.

Per serving: 90 calories, 2 g total fat, 1 g saturated fat, 7 g protein, 13 g carbohydrates, 2 g dietary fiber, 200 mg sodium

MINT

Whether as a soothing tea or part of a recipe, mint has long been part of both the cuisine and the medicinal culture of societies as diverse as those in the Middle East, India, and Europe. The origins of mint are honored in a Greek myth in which the plant was originally a nymph (Minthe) who was transformed into a plant by Persephone, who was jealous of the affections that her husband Hades was showing to Minthe. While Hades could not reverse the spell that his wife cast, he did impart Minthe with a sweet smell, so when she was walked upon in the garden, her aroma would be delightful to the senses.

Mint contains a phytonutrient called perillyl alcohol, which has been shown in studies on animals to be preventive in the formation of some cancers. All mint varieties contain menthol, a compound that helps digestion and has antiseptic properties.

Mint's fresh flavor is best when the leaves are left uncooked. Adding raw mint leaves to sautéed vegetables, grilled fish, and roasted poultry and lamb dishes toward the end of the cooking process imparts a fresh flavor to any meal.

Whenever possible, choose fresh mint over the dried herb since it is superior in flavor. The leaves of fresh mint should look vibrant and be a rich green color. They should be free from dark spots or yellowing.

To store fresh mint leaves, carefully wrap them in a damp paper towel and place inside a loosely closed plastic bag. Store in the refrigerator, where they should keep fresh for several days.

GINGER AND
HONEY SMOOTHIE

Ginger has been used in Chinese herbal medicine for
centuries as a stimulating tonic for the digestive system.
Combined with the yogurt, which supports good digestive
health, this is an ideal drink for the middle of the day.

SERVES 2

1	cup ice cubes
1	piece (1 inch/2.5 cm) fresh ginger, peeled and sliced
6	ounces (170 g) fat-free plain yogurt
1	cup (240 ml) fat-free milk, oat milk, or almond milk
2	tablespoons (30 ml) honey
$\frac{1}{4}$	teaspoon ground cinnamon, plus extra for dusting

Place the ice in a blender or food processor and pulse to crush the ice. Add the ginger, yogurt, milk, honey, and $\frac{1}{4}$ teaspoon cinnamon. Blend until smooth. Pour into tall glasses and dust with extra cinnamon before serving.

Per serving: 150 calories, 0 g total fat, 0 g saturated fat, 8 g protein, 31 g carbohydrates, 0 g dietary fiber, 105 mg sodium

VIRGIN MARY

My husband, Leonard, is known for his flavorful Bloody Mary made with Clamato juice and aquavit. However, this nonalcoholic version would be delicious served with the Smoked Trout Salad a la Grècque (page 92) to make a healthy lunch.

SERVES 2

1	cup (240 ml) tomato juice or Clamato juice
2	tablespoons (30 ml) lemon juice
	Pinch of celery salt
4-8	drops Worcestershire sauce
	Ice cubes
½	teaspoon grated horseradish, preferably fresh
2-6	drops Tabasco sauce
	Kosher salt and freshly ground black pepper
2	celery ribs
2	lemon wedges

In a large shaker, combine the tomato juice, lemon juice, celery salt, and Worcestershire sauce. Add ice cubes, shake well, and strain into old-fashioned glasses containing ice. Season with the horseradish, Tabasco, and salt and pepper. Garnish with the celery ribs and lemon wedges to serve.

Per serving: 35 calories, 0 g total fat, 0 g saturated fat, 1 g protein, 8 g carbohydrates, 1 g dietary fiber, 460 mg sodium

SPICED MANGO LASSI

Lassis are popular Indian beverages made with yogurt, and this mango version is a good way to include whole fruit, which is a great source of fiber. Serve chilled.

SERVES 2

12	ounces (340 g) fat-free plain yogurt
	Juice of 1 lemon
2	cups sliced mango
$\frac{1}{2}$	cup (120 ml) cold water
2	tablespoons (30 ml) honey
$\frac{1}{8}$	teaspoon ground cardamom
	Pinch of chili powder (optional)
9-10	ice cubes

Place the yogurt, lemon juice, mango, water, and honey in a blender or food processor and blend until smooth. Season with the cardamom and chili powder, if using. Add the ice and blend until frothy. Serve.

Per serving: 250 calories, 0 g total fat, 0 g saturated fat, 8 g protein, 62 g carbohydrates, 3 g dietary fiber, 110 mg sodium

YOGURT

Yogurt is milk that has had beneficial bacteria added to it, traditionally *Lactobacillus bulgaricus* and *Streptococcus thermophilus.* The bacteria cause the milk to ferment and thicken, and they give yogurt its characteristic tangy taste.

Yogurt was originally produced to extend the keeping qualities of milk, but now it is enjoyed simply for its taste and versatility in cooking. Yogurt can be made from whole or fat-free milk. Over the past 10 years, new bacteria have been used in yogurt-making to create "bio yogurts," which are reputed to aid digestion. When choosing yogurt, look for brands that contain "live" cultures and be sure to use them before the expiration date.

Natural yogurt can be added to fresh fruit and cereal for breakfast. It can be used to make dips, salad dressings, and a garnish for soups. Yogurt adds creamy taste and texture to sauces and curries. It can also be a substitute for cream or ice cream or a topping for fresh fruit, meringues, or cakes.

BEET JEWEL

Not only high in folate, red beets contain phytochemicals including betacyanin, thought to help prevent cancer. Look for beets with fresh-looking greens attached, reserve when juicing the root, and sauté them with a little olive oil and garlic as a vegetable dish or keep the beet greens for the next soup you make. There's a tradition that says cooked beet greens relieve the discomfort of women's menstrual cycles.

SERVES 2

4	raw beets, tops removed
1	large English cucumber
4	limes, peeled
	Crushed ice
2	lime wedges

Feed the beets, cucumber, and limes through a juice extractor. Pour into glasses containing ice and garnish with lime wedges. Serve.

Per serving: 130 calories, 0.5 g total fat, 0 g saturated fat, 5 g protein, 34 g carbohydrates, 10 g dietary fiber, 135 mg sodium

OTHER VARIETIES OF GREENS INCLUDE BROCCOLI RABE, BABY SPINACH, AND PEA SHOOTS.

MELON AGUA FRESCA

A refreshing alternative to iced tea or lemonade at a summertime party, serve this in a large jar with a ladle so guests can help themselves.

SERVES 4

1	very ripe red seedless watermelon, about 6 pounds (3 kg)
	Juice of 3 limes
1	cup fresh mint leaves, crushed
2	cups (480 ml) sparkling water
2	limes, thinly sliced
	Fresh mint sprigs

Per serving: 120 calories, 0 g total fat, 0 g saturated fat, 2 g protein, 40 g carbohydrates, 4 g dietary fiber, 40 mg sodium

Cut the watermelon in half and scoop the flesh into a large bowl. Working in batches, puree the watermelon in a blender or food processor. As each batch is ready, transfer to another large bowl. Add the lime juice and mint to the puree and stir to combine. Cover and set aside at room temperature for 1 hour to let the flavors develop.

Strain the watermelon mixture through a medium-mesh sieve into a wide-mouth jar or pitcher. It's okay to have some of the pulp in the agua fresca. Add the sparkling water and lime slices. Ladle into glasses and garnish with mint sprigs. Serve.

AVOCADO, PAPAYA, AND PINK GRAPEFRUIT WITH MAPLE DRESSING

This is a particularly pretty salad that is also particularly good for you! Papayas contain the enzyme papain, which is good for digestion, and are an excellent source of vitamin C as well as a good source of vitamin E and beta-carotene, three very powerful antioxidants. Avocados are a good source of monounsaturated fat, potassium, and vitamin E, and pink grapefruit is an excellent source of vitamin C.

SERVES 4 TO 6

2	pink grapefruit
1	medium papaya
2	firm, ripe avocados, cut in half, pitted, and peeled
	Juice of 1 lemon
2	tablespoons (30 ml) pure maple syrup
	Juice of 3 limes
	Freshly ground pink peppercorns (optional)

Per serving (based on 4 servings): 260 calories, 16 g total fat, 2.5 g saturated fat, 3 g protein, 34 g carbohydrates, 8 g dietary fiber, 15 mg sodium

Using a very sharp knife, remove all the skin and pith from the grapefruit. Slide the knife down one side of each fruit segment, then cut down the other side and gently pull out the segment and place in a bowl. Peel the papaya, cut in half, and remove the seeds. Slice into pieces about 2½ inches by ½ inch wide (6.5 cm by 1.3 cm). Add to the bowl and toss to combine.

Slice the avocados lengthwise into ½-inch (1.3 cm) slices and pour the lemon juice over the slices. Add to the fruit mixture.

In a small saucepan, warm the maple syrup and lime juice, whisking to combine; set aside to cool. Toss the fruits together and drizzle with the dressing. Season with the peppercorns, if using. Serve.

POMEGRANATE WITH LIME, LOW-FAT RICOTTA, AND HONEY

The pomegranate has recently been acclaimed for its health benefits, in particular, for its disease-fighting antioxidant potential. Antioxidants can help to reduce free-radical damage to our bodies' cellular materials, which may be linked to degenerative illnesses, such as cardiovascular disease, cancer, or even aging itself.

SERVES 4

4	pomegranates
	Juice of 2 limes
1	cup (230 g) low-fat ricotta cheese
4	teaspoons (20 ml) honey, such as chestnut or lavender
	Lime wedges (optional)

Per serving: 190 calories, 3.5 g total fat, 2 g saturated fat, 9 g protein, 37 g carbohydrates, 1 g dietary fiber, 160 mg sodium

Crack open the pomegranates by pressing down on them with the heel of your hand (or halve with a sharp knife). Hold over a bowl to catch the juices and dig out the seeds with a small spoon. Discard the skin and the white membrane.

Toss the pomegranate seeds with the lime juice and refrigerate for 1 hour, or until chilled. Divide the ricotta among 4 shallow bowls, spoon one-quarter of the pomegranate seeds into each bowl, and drizzle with the honey. Serve with a few lime wedges, if desired.

BAKED OMELET
WITH SQUASH

Eggs are a good source of high-quality protein, and combining eggs with squash in this dish adds health benefits of beta-carotene, known for its possible anti-inflammatory effects. On top of that, adding walnuts gives this recipe a boost of omega-3 fatty acids.

SERVES 6

1	small butternut squash, about 1 pound (450 g), peeled, seeded, and cut into chunks
1	tablespoon (15 ml) extra-virgin olive oil
2	small leeks, cleaned and chopped (white and light green parts only)
6	large eggs, lightly beaten
1/4	cup (60 ml) milk
1/4	cup finely chopped fresh dill, plus extra for garnish
1/4	cup finely chopped walnuts
	Ground nutmeg
	Kosher salt and freshly ground black pepper
2	tablespoons dried currants
	Fat-free plain yogurt, for drizzling

Per serving: 190 calories, 11 g total fat, 2.5 g saturated fat, 9 g protein, 16 g carbohydrates, 2 g dietary fiber, 105 mg sodium

Place 1 inch (2.5 cm) of water in a saucepan and bring to a simmer over medium heat. Place the squash in a steamer basket and add to the pan. Cover and steam until tender, about 8 minutes. Transfer to a large bowl. Mash with a fork and set aside to cool.

Preheat the oven to 325°F (160°C). Add the oil to a 6-cup (1.5 liter) gratin dish. Add the leeks and toss to coat. Bake for about 10 minutes, or until softened; set aside.

Gradually mix the eggs into the squash. Stir in the milk, 1/4 cup of the dill, and walnuts. Season with nutmeg and salt and pepper. Pour the mixture into the gratin dish and sprinkle with the currants. Bake for about 45 minutes, or until set. Cut into squares and sprinkle with additional dill. Serve warm drizzled with yogurt.

BORSCHT RING

I served this at a Russian meal with a wonderful stroganoff main course. It conjures up memories of legendary Russian centenarians, who probably have eaten many beets over the years. It would make a pretty accompaniment to poached chicken or salmon.

SERVES 8 TO 10

1   jar (32 ounces/1 liter) borscht, prefer-
    ably Manischewitz

1   jar (16 ounces/450 g) pickled beets

4   envelopes unflavored gelatin

1   bunch watercress, leaves only

1   cup (230 g) fat-free sour cream

3   tablespoons finely chopped fresh dill

1   tablespoon finely chopped fresh
    chives

Per serving (based on 8 servings): 120 calories, 0 g total fat, 0 g saturated fat, 6 g protein, 24 g carbohydrates, 3 g dietary fiber, 390 mg sodium

Strain the borscht into a large saucepan. Scoop ¼ cup (60 ml) of the liquid into a small bowl and set aside. Transfer the solids to a blender or food processor; puree and add to the saucepan. Puree the pickled beets and add to the pan.

Sprinkle the gelatin over the reserved ¼ cup (60 ml) liquid and let stand for 5 minutes to soften. Heat the borscht until it starts to steam. Stir in the dissolved gelatin until well combined. Remove from the heat and pour into a lightly oiled 6-cup (1.5-liter) ring mold. Cover and refrigerate for at least 5 hours or overnight.

To serve, unmold the salad onto a serving platter and fill the center with watercress leaves. In a small bowl, mix the sour cream, dill, and chives and serve with the watercress as the dressing.

SPINACH AND HERB SOUFFLÉ WITH AVOCADO WATERCRESS COULIS

The word *soufflé* is a revered cooking term, but it is really very easy to make and so enjoyable to eat. This soufflé would be ideal served with steamed asparagus for a light lunch. Spinach is a nutrient-dense food, which contains good amounts of vitamins A, C, and K and folate, a water-soluble B vitamin known among many other functions for cell protection.

SERVES 4

2	tablespoons (30 g) butter, plus extra for the baking dish
¼	cup finely grated Parmesan cheese
1	cup (240 ml) milk or goat milk, if available
1	small onion, peeled and studded with 2 cloves
3	tablespoons unbleached all-purpose flour
½	cup mixed chopped fresh herbs, such as chives, tarragon, flat-leaf parsley, and chervil
1	pound baby spinach leaves, lightly cooked, squeezed dry, and roughly chopped
2	tablespoons (30 g) crumbled goat cheese
2	large egg yolks
	Kosher salt and freshly ground black pepper
6	large egg whites
	Avocado Watercress Coulis (recipe follows)

Preheat the oven to 350°F (180°C). Lightly butter an 8-cup (2-liter) soufflé dish and coat with the Parmesan.

Heat the milk and onion in a small saucepan over medium heat until hot (do not let the milk boil). Set aside to infuse for 10 minutes, then discard the onion.

Melt 2 tablespoons of the butter in a medium saucepan over low heat. Add the flour and cook, stirring, until the butter foams. Whisk in the warm milk and cook, stirring, until the sauce thickens. Add the herbs, spinach, and goat cheese. Beat in the egg yolks, one at a time; cook, stirring, for 1 minute. Season with salt and pepper. Set aside.

In a large bowl, beat the egg whites with a handheld electric mixer until stiff peaks form. Fold one-quarter of the whites into the spinach mixture to lighten it. Fold the spinach mixture into the remaining whites. Transfer to the soufflé dish. Bake for 40 minutes, or until the soufflé has risen and is golden brown on top. Serve immediately with the coulis.

AVOCADO WATERCRESS COULIS

This can be made ahead and refrigerated for up to 3 hours before serving.

SERVES 4

¼	bunch watercress, leaves only
1	avocado, pitted, peeled, and coarsely chopped
	Juice of 2 lemons
1	tablespoon (15 ml) extra-virgin olive oil

In a blender; combine the watercress, avocado, lemon juice, and oil. Blend until smooth. If you prefer a thinner sauce, blend in a little water to reach the desired consistency.

Per serving (with coulis): 380 calories, 24 g total fat, 10 g saturated fat, 18 g protein, 28 g carbohydrates, 9 g dietary fiber, 520 mg sodium

GREEN THUMBS

I never chop herbs with a knife, because their cut edges turn brown or even black. The best way to add fresh herbs to a dish is simply to tear the leaves with clean fingers. The flavor comes out very nicely, and your hands smell delicious afterward!

Even though bouquets of freshly harvested herbs do well for a few days when kept in a vase, like flowers, they last longer—and stay crisper—when gently wrapped in a damp dish or paper towel and then placed in a plastic bag and stored in the refrigerator's drawer.

GAZPACHO

Gazpacho is a Mediterranean vegetable soup that typically combines tomato, cucumber, and sweet pepper along with olive oil, onion, garlic, and vinegar. I serve my gazpacho with freshly made croutons and chopped red onions, green and red peppers, corn, and celery presented in individual bowls, which gives guests a choice of the extra flavor in their soup.

SERVES 4 TO 6

SOUP

10	ripe tomatoes, cut into quarters
1	medium red onion, peeled and chopped
1	garlic clove, peeled
1	cucumber, peeled, halved lengthwise, and seeded
1	tablespoon (15 ml) rice wine vinegar
1	teaspoon superfine (caster) sugar

CROUTONS

3	slices whole-wheat bread
1	tablespoon (15 ml) garlic-flavored extra-virgin olive oil

CONDIMENTS

2	celery ribs, finely diced
1	red or green bell pepper, finely diced
1	large red onion, peeled and finely diced
	Kernels from 1 ear of corn

For the soup: Put the tomatoes, onion, garlic, and cucumber in a food processor or blender and puree with the vinegar and sugar. Transfer to a pitcher, cover, and refrigerate until chilled, at least 1 hour.

For the croutons: Cut the bread into small squares. Heat the oil in a medium nonstick skillet over medium heat. Toast the bread pieces, stirring until they are golden on all sides.

Serve the soup in individual bowls with small bowls of the condiments and croutons for guests to serve themselves.

Per serving (based on 4 servings): 240 calories, 6 g total fat, 1 g saturated fat, 9 g protein, 43 g carbohydrates, 10 g dietary fiber, 150 mg sodium

CORN FRITTERS

Fritters are traditionally fried as a ball, but I make mine flat as a pancake. I serve them as a vegetable course with roast chicken. My son Gary loves the breakfast version with maple syrup. Corn is rich in fiber and carotenoids that give yellow corn its color. These nutrients are generally preventive against heart disease and cancer.

MAKES 18

2   teaspoons (10 ml) light extra-virgin olive oil

1   garlic clove, peeled and minced

1   small onion, peeled and minced

1   recipe Plain Pancakes (page 39) or Buckwheat Silver Dollar Pancakes (page 42)

1   small can kernel corn

1   small can creamed corn (see note)

Per fritter: 70 calories, 2.5 g total fat, 0 g saturated fat, 3 g protein, 12 g carbohydrates, 0 g dietary fiber, 105 mg sodium

Preheat the oven to 250°F (120°C).

Heat 1 teaspoon (5 ml) of the oil in a large non-stick skillet over medium heat and sauté the garlic and onions until soft, about 1 minute. Remove from the heat.

In a large bowl, mix the pancake mixture with the cooked onions and garlic and the canned corn kernels and creamed corn.

Heat the remaining 1 teaspoon (5 ml) oil in the large nonstick skillet over medium-high heat. Drop heaping tablespoons of the batter into the pan 2 inches (5 cm) apart. Fry until golden brown, 1 to 2 minutes on each side. Transfer to paper towels to drain, place on a plate, and keep warm in the oven. Repeat with the remaining batter, adding more oil as needed and reducing the heat to medium if the fritters brown too quickly.

NOTE: Look for canned cream corn that has no additives, such as the Butter Kernal brand.

VARIATION

To make these as a breakfast dish, simply omit the garlic and onion and cook as per the recipe.

LENTIL SOUP

Lentils, a small but nutritionally mighty member of the legume family, are a very good source of cholesterol-lowering fiber and protein. This soup was inspired by a recipe in Jane Brody's *Good Food Book*.

SERVES 4

2	tablespoons (30 ml) extra-virgin olive oil
3	garlic cloves, peeled
1	large onion, peeled and minced
3	carrots, peeled and coarsely grated
$3/4$	teaspoon minced fresh marjoram
$3/4$	teaspoon minced fresh thyme
1	can (28 ounces/800 g) tomatoes in juice, coarsely chopped
7	cups (1.7 liters) Basic Vegetable Stock (page 139) or chicken broth
$1 1/2$	cups dried lentils, picked over and rinsed
$1/2$	teaspoon kosher salt
	Freshly ground black pepper
$3/4$	cup (180 ml) dry white wine
$1/3$	cup chopped fresh flat-leaf parsley
4	ounces (115 g) low-fat Cheddar cheese, shredded

Heat the oil in a large pot over medium heat. Add the garlic, onion, carrots, marjoram, and thyme. Cook, stirring occasionally, for 5 minutes, or until the onion is translucent. Add the tomatoes, stock, and lentils.

Bring to a boil, reduce the heat, cover, and simmer for 50 minutes, or until the lentils are tender. Remove the garlic, mash, and stir into the soup. Season with salt and pepper. Add the wine and parsley and allow to simmer for a few minutes more. Ladle into bowls and sprinkle with the cheese.

Per serving: 450 calories, 12 g total fat, 3 g saturated fat, 30 g protein, 52 g carbohydrates, 17 g dietary fiber, 830 mg sodium

ROASTED TOMATO SOUP

The redder the tomato, the higher its level of lycopene and beta-carotene, which is converted into vitamin A in the body. Serve this delicious soup with a drizzle of good-quality balsamic vinegar.

SERVES 4

4	pounds (2 kg) very ripe red tomatoes
4	garlic cloves, peeled and minced
2	shallots, peeled and minced
3	tablespoons (45 ml) balsamic vinegar
1/2	teaspoon kosher salt, plus extra for seasoning
1/2	teaspoon freshly ground black pepper, plus extra for seasoning
1/4	cup (60 ml) extra-virgin olive oil
1	teaspoon sugar (optional)

Per serving: 230 calories, 15 g total fat, 2 g saturated fat, 4 g protein, 24 g carbohydrates, 6 g dietary fiber, 290 mg sodium

Preheat the oven to 400°F (200°C).

Cut the tomatoes in half crosswise and place, cut side down, in an ovenproof dish. Sprinkle with the garlic, shallots, 3 tablespoons vinegar, 1/2 teaspoon salt, and 1/2 teaspoon pepper. Pour the oil over all and roast for 40 minutes, or until the tomatoes collapse.

Transfer to a blender or food processor and puree. Strain through a fine-mesh sieve into a saucepan, pressing on the solids with the back of a large spoon. Cook for 4 minutes over medium-low heat. Stir in the sugar, if using, and season with salt and pepper.

Ladle into bowls and drizzle with additional vinegar, if desired.

CARROT AND PAPAYA SOUP

Carrots are full of beta-carotene, and papaya contains papain, an enzyme that helps to reduce inflammation, making it a wonderful tonic for the skin. Papaya seeds have a surprising peppery flavor. If you have a juicer, make your own carrot juice; otherwise, look for fresh juice at the store.

SERVES 4

1   ripe papaya

4   cups (1 liter) carrot juice

4   teaspoons (20 g) fat-free sour cream (optional)

Per serving: 100 calories, 0 g total fat, 0 g saturated fat, 2 g protein, 21 g carbohydrates, 1 g dietary fiber, 150 mg sodium

Halve the papaya and scoop out the seeds, reserving 1 tablespoon of the seeds. Peel the papaya and cut into chunks; place in a blender. Add the carrot juice and the reserved seeds. Blend until smooth. Pour into soup bowls and top with the sour cream, if using.

ANDREW WEIL'S CURRIED CAULIFLOWER SOUP

A world-renowned pioneer in integrative medicine, Dr. Andrew Weil has made a tremendous impact on the ways in which people view healing and health. I am honored that he has given me some recipes for my book. Garnished with chopped cilantro and caramelized onion rings, this soup is delicious hot or cold.

SERVES 4 TO 6

SOUP

1	tablespoon (15 ml) grape seed oil or canola oil
1	medium onion, peeled and sliced
1	tablespoon hot curry powder
1	tablespoon sweet curry powder
1	teaspoon ground turmeric
	Kosher salt
1	large head cauliflower, separated into florets
4–6	cups (1–1.5 liters) Basic Vegetable Stock (page 139)
¾	cup cashews
¾	cup (180 ml) water
1	tablespoon light brown sugar
1	cup cilantro sprigs, chopped

For the soup: Heat the oil in a large pot over medium heat. Add the onion and cook, stirring, until translucent. Add the curry powders, turmeric, and salt to taste. Cook for 1 minute. Add the cauliflower and stir to mix well. Add enough stock to cover the cauliflower; bring to a boil and simmer for 10 minutes, or until the cauliflower is just tender.

Place the cashews in a blender and grind to a fine powder. Add the water and blend on high speed for 2 minutes.

Using an immersion blender or food processor, puree the cauliflower mixture. Add the cashew mixture and sugar. Add more stock or water if the soup is too thick. Bring to a simmer and season with more salt, if needed.

Sprinkle the onion rings on top of the soup along with the cilantro as a garnish.

ONION RINGS

1   large onion, peeled and sliced into rings
2   teaspoons (10 ml) extra-virgin olive oil
    Kosher salt and freshly ground black pepper

For the onion rings: Preheat the oven to 250°F (120°C). In a bowl, toss together the onion rings and oil. Season with salt and pepper. Spread the onions on a baking sheet and bake until lightly browned, moving them about as necessary.

Per serving (based on 4 servings): 320 calories, 18 g total fat, 3 g saturated fat, 10 g protein, 36 g carbohydrates, 9 g dietary fiber, 160 mg sodium

CURRY

Curry is a dried powder of a readily available blend of spices that is a Western approximation of Indian spice blends, and it typically contains turmeric, coriander, chilies, cumin, mustard, ginger, fenugreek, garlic, cloves, salt, and any number of other spices.

Turmeric, a main ingredient in curry powder, is the traditional curry spice that gives many Indian dishes their golden hue, and it is a powerful anti-inflammatory and antioxidant shown by scientists to protect the liver against a variety of toxic substances.

Usually thought of as just a coloring agent by Westerners, turmeric is a close cousin to ginger and has been considered a potent medicinal plant in Asia for thousands of years. It is used by Indian doctors to treat everything from sprains to jaundice.

Recently, one of the spice's active ingredients, curcumin, has piqued the interest of Western researchers. In large doses, it has been shown to be as effective as cortisone for the acute inflammation caused by arthritis. But one of the most promising uses of curcumin may be in treating cancer.

Curry powder offers a pleasant, easy way to add these vitally important substances to one's diet. A good teaspoon of curry powder (yes, the kind in the supermarket) per pound of meat in any recipe will turn that dish into a mild "curry." Or use in vegetable dishes. Or simply keep curry powder at the table and sprinkle it lightly onto your food or onto soups or dips—it is already roasted.

AVOCADO HERB SALAD

The creamy, delicately flavored avocado needs little enhancement, but to appreciate its flavor fully, the avocado must be ripe. The health benefits of avocado are many, providing good fats, potassium, and folate, essential nutrients for heart health.

SERVES 4 TO 6

2 tablespoons (30 ml) avocado oil or extra-virgin olive oil

Juice of 2 limes

Kosher salt and freshly ground black pepper

2 ripe, firm avocados

2 limes, peeled and cut into segments

1 cup fresh basil leaves

1 Belgian endive, leaves separated

In a small bowl, whisk together the oil and lime juice. Season with salt and pepper. Halve, pit, and peel the avocados. Slice lengthwise and arrange on a serving dish with the lime segments, basil, and endive. Drizzle with the dressing and serve.

Per serving (based on 4 servings): 230 calories, 21 g total fat, 2.5 g saturated fat, 3 g protein, 14 g carbohydrates, 8 g dietary fiber, 40 mg sodium

SWEET AND SOUR CUCUMBER SALAD

My mother, Mimi Hausner, frequently made this Austrian salad to accompany Wiener schnitzel, the Austrian version of veal Milanese, as well as roast chicken or poached salmon. It cools the palate refreshingly and enhances the flavor of the protein.

SERVES 4

2	large dark green cucumbers
1	tablespoon salt
1	small yellow onion, peeled and finely chopped
2	scallions (white part only), finely chopped
½	bunch fresh dill leaves, chopped
½	cup (120 ml) rice wine vinegar
¼	cup (60 ml) water
1	tablespoon (15 ml) canola oil
1	tablespoon superfine (caster) sugar

Per serving: 70 calories, 4 g total fat, 0 g saturated fat, 1 g protein, 10 g carbohydrates, 2 g dietary fiber, 590 mg sodium

Peel the cucumbers and cut in half lengthwise. Use a spoon or melon scoop to remove the seeds. Thinly slice the cucumbers using a mandoline or the slicing window of a grater and place in a medium glass bowl. Sprinkle with the salt and stir to combine. Lay a sheet of plastic wrap directly on the cucumbers and top with a small plate that fits inside the bowl. Place a heavy can on the plate to weigh down the cucumbers. Refrigerate for 1 to 2 hours to let the juice seep from the cucumber slices.

Transfer the cucumbers to a colander and rinse thoroughly under cold water; drain. Use the palms of your hands to squeeze out the excess liquid from the cucumbers, pressing as hard as you can. Place the cucumbers in a large bowl. Add the onion, scallions, and dill; toss to combine.

In a small bowl, mix the vinegar, water, oil, and sugar until the sugar dissolves. Pour over the cucumber mixture and mix well. Cover and refrigerate until serving time; stir before serving.

COLESLAW

Cabbage belongs to the Cruciferae family of vegetables along with kale, broccoli, collards, and Brussels sprouts. This sweet coleslaw, which contains raisins, is a favorite of my daughter-in-law Laura and is a perfect side dish with barbecued ribs, chicken, or trout.

SERVES 6 TO 8

1	head green or Savoy cabbage
2	large carrots, peeled and coarsely grated
1	cup raisins
¾	cup (170 g) fat-free mayonnaise
1	teaspoon mustard powder
1	teaspoon celery seeds
4	tablespoons (60 ml) rice wine vinegar
1	tablespoon sugar

Per serving (based on 6 servings): 170 calories, 1.5 g total fat, 0 g saturated fat, 3 g protein, 39 g carbohydrates, 7 g dietary fiber, 310 mg sodium

Discard the coarse outer cabbage leaves. Cut the cabbage into 2-inch (5 cm) wedges and remove the core. Slice the wedges very thinly crosswise. Transfer to a large bowl and add the carrots and raisins.

In a small bowl, mix the mayonnaise, mustard, celery seeds, vinegar, and sugar; thin with a little water, if desired. Pour over the coleslaw and toss to coat. Let stand for 15 minutes or chill for up to 2 hours to let the flavors develop before serving.

VARIATION
For an Asian twist, add some chopped fresh cilantro.

ASIAN SHRIMP OR CHICKEN SALAD

This salad is equally good whether it's made with shrimp or chicken, and sprinkling the crispy rice noodles on top adds a surprising crunch and makes a lovely presentation.

SERVES 6

DRESSING

- 1/3 cup (80 ml) rice wine vinegar
- 3/4 cup (180 ml) thick teriyaki sauce
- 2 tablespoons (30 ml) toasted sesame oil
- 2 tablespoons (30 ml) lemon juice
- 2 tablespoons toasted sesame seeds
- 1 tablespoon (15 ml) honey or sugar
- 2 garlic cloves, peeled and finely chopped

SHRIMP OR CHICKEN

- 1/4 cup (60 ml) low-sodium soy sauce
- 1 teaspoon peeled and grated fresh ginger
- 1 teaspoon grated lemon zest
     Juice of 2 lemons
- 1 1/2 pounds (680 g) medium shrimp, peeled and deveined or 3 medium skinless, boneless chicken breasts, about 1 1/4 pounds (570 g)
- 1 tablespoon (15 ml) extra-virgin olive oil

SALAD

- 1 small head Savoy or Chinese cabbage, finely chopped
- 2 celery ribs, strings removed and sliced on the diagonal
- 4 scallions, finely sliced (white and green parts)
- 1 cup bean sprouts
- 2 carrots, peeled and julienned
- 1/2 cup whole or chopped unsalted cashews
- 1 can (8 ounces/230 g) sliced water chestnuts, drained and sliced into small chunks
- 1 1/2 cups fresh cilantro leaves
- 4 ounces (115 g) dried rice noodles
- 3/4 cup crispy rice noodles (optional)

Per serving (with shrimp): 480 calories, 21 g total fat, 3.5 g saturated fat, 31 g protein, 45 g carbohydrates, 6 g dietary fiber, 1,520 mg sodium

For the dressing: Whisk the vinegar, teriyaki sauce, sesame oil, lemon juice, sesame seeds, honey or sugar, and garlic in a small bowl. Cover and refrigerate.

For the shrimp: In a shallow dish, mix the soy sauce, ginger, lemon zest, and lemon juice. Add the shrimp and stir to coat. Let stand for 10 minutes.

Heat the oil in a large nonstick skillet over medium-high heat. Add the shrimp and cook, turning once, until pink, about 4 minutes. Transfer to a plate.

For the salad: In a large bowl, mix the cabbage, celery, scallions, bean sprouts, carrots, cashews, water chestnuts, and cilantro. Add the dressing and toss to combine.

Bring a large pot of water to a boil. Add the dried rice noodles and cook for 4 to 5 minutes, or until al dente; drain.

Arrange the salad in the center of a platter and top with the shrimp. Place the rice noodles around the salad and present scattered with the crispy noodles on top, if desired.

If using chicken: In a shallow dish, mix the soy sauce, ginger, lemon zest, and lemon juice. Add the chicken and stir to coat. Let stand for 10 minutes. Heat the oil in large nonstick skillet over medium heat. Add the chicken and cook, turning once, about 6 minutes, until just cooked through. Transfer to a cutting board and cut the chicken into strips. Once the salad is arranged, top with the chicken strips.

EXCEPTIONAL TUNA SALAD

I add green pickle relish and rice wine vinegar to my tuna fish salad, which seems to add an extra zing to its flavor.

SERVES 6

2	cans (7 ounce/225 g each) tuna packed in water
1	cup chopped celery
½	cup (115 g) fat-free mayonnaise
1	tablespoon (15 ml) rice wine vinegar
1	tablespoon (15 g) green pickle relish
½	lemon, juiced
	Pinch of ground cloves
	Garlic and onion powder to taste (optional)

Drain the tuna and place in a medium bowl, gently breaking into pieces with a fork. Add the celery.

In a small bowl, mix the mayonnaise then slowly add the vinegar while stirring. Add the relish, lemon juice, and cloves. Spoon over the tuna and mix to combine. Season with garlic and onion powder, if using.

Per serving: 100 calories, 2.5 g total fat, 0.5 g saturated fat, 14 g protein, 5 g carbohydrates, 0 g dietary fiber, 410 mg sodium

POTATO SALAD

This was a dish my mother made, and to this day it is a favorite of mine. I remember her using a piece of lemon rind to stop the caraway seeds from popping all over the board as she chopped them. A small amount of potato salad with roast chicken or wurst is a very traditional Viennese dish.

SERVES 6

2½ pounds (1.2 kg) medium red boiling potatoes

1 teaspoon kosher salt, plus extra for seasoning

1 teaspoon plus 1 tablespoon caraway seeds

4 tablespoons (60 ml) cider vinegar

3 large celery ribs, strings, removed and finely chopped (see note)

Grated zest of 1 lemon

1 cup (230 g) fat-free mayonnaise or fat-free Greek-style yogurt

2 tablespoons (30 ml) honey mustard

1 tablespoon (15 g) green pickle relish

Freshly ground black pepper

Chopped fresh flat-leaf parsley or scallions

Per serving: 190 calories, 2 g total fat, 0 g saturated fat, 4 g protein, 40 g carbohydrates, 5 g dietary fiber, 560 mg sodium

Place the potatoes in a large saucepan and add enough cold water to cover by 1 inch (2.5 cm). Stir in 1 teaspoon salt and 1 teaspoon caraway seeds. Cover and simmer until just tender, about 15 to 30 minutes, depending on the size of the potatoes. Drain and set aside until just warm.

Rub a sharp knife with a little oil to keep it from sticking and cut the potatoes into ⅓-inch-thick (0.8 cm) slices. Place in a large bowl and immediately toss gently with 3 tablespoons (45 ml) of the vinegar. Add the celery.

Using a mortar and pestle, crush together the lemon zest and remaining 1 tablespoon caraway seeds or chop on a board. Place in a small bowl and stir in the mayonnaise or yogurt, mustard, relish, and the remaining 1 tablespoon (15 ml) vinegar. Pour over the potatoes and celery and gently toss to combine. Season with salt and pepper. Garnish with the parsley or scallions. Serve chilled or at room temperature.

DESTRINGING CELERY

To remove the strings from celery ribs, cut across the base of the stalk just above where it joins the base. Using the flat side of your knife, you can lift several strings at once and pull upward toward the top of the stalk. You can destring one stalk in two or three such strokes.

ANDREW WEIL'S GREEN BEAN SALAD

Dr. Andrew Weil is a consultant to the Origins brand. His work with natural ingredients is very well known. The vitamin K provided by green beans—a spectacular 122 percent of the Daily Value in 1 cup—is important for maintaining strong bones.

SERVES 4 TO 6

1   pound (450 g) haricots verts or other thin green beans

2   tablespoons (30 ml) extra-virgin olive oil

2   garlic cloves, peeled and finely minced

4   strips lemon zest

2   Turkish bay leaves or ½ California bay leaf

    Kosher salt

Per serving (based on 4 servings): 100 calories, 7 g total fat, 1 g saturated fat, 2 g protein, 9 g carbohydrates, 4 g dietary fiber, 35 mg sodium

Bring a large pot of water to a boil. Add the beans and cook for 5 minutes, or until bright green and just crunchy-tender. Do not overcook. Drain and rinse with cold water. Drain and pat dry. Transfer to a large bowl.

Add the oil, garlic, lemon zest, and bay leaves. Toss to coat and season with salt. Cover and let stand at room temperature for several hours to allow the flavors to blend. Remove and discard the bay leaves and zest. Serve.

SHAVED VEGETABLE SALAD

A mandoline is a wonderful tool for preparing fresh vegetables and hard fruits in salads so they are ribbon thin. This simple but refreshing salad would be delicious served with fresh mozzarella cheese.

SERVES 4 TO 6

2	heads Belgian endive
3	celery ribs plus 1 cup pale celery leaves
1	fennel bulb, trimmed
2	Granny Smith apples, halved and cored
¼	cup raisins
3	tablespoons (45 ml) extra-virgin olive oil
2	tablespoons (30 ml) fresh lemon juice
	Freshly ground black pepper

Using a mandoline, V-Slicer, or large sharp knife, very thinly slice the endive, celery ribs, fennel, and apples crosswise. Place in a large bowl and add the celery leaves and raisins. Sprinkle with the oil and lemon juice and toss to coat. Season with the pepper and serve.

Per serving (based on 4 servings): 190 calories, 11 g total fat, 1.5 g saturated fat, 2 g protein, 24 g carbohydrates, 6 g dietary fiber, 60 mg sodium

POACHED LEEKS WITH WALNUT VINAIGRETTE

In the same family as onions and garlic but with a more delicate and sweeter flavor, leeks possess many of the same nutrients but in lesser concentrations. Combined with walnuts—an excellent source of omega-3 essential fatty acids—this leek recipe provides a good combination of protective nutrients for the cardiovascular and immune systems.

SERVES 4

1	teaspoon kosher salt, plus extra for seasoning
8	small leeks, cleaned
½	cup walnut halves
1	teaspoon minced fresh rosemary leaves
¼	cup (60 ml) walnut oil
2	tablespoons (30 ml) champagne vinegar
2	tablespoons finely chopped fresh flat-leaf parsley
	Freshly ground black pepper

Per serving: 320 calories, 22 g total fat, 2 g saturated fat, 5 g protein, 28 g carbohydrates, 4 g dietary fiber, 540 mg sodium

Bring a pot of water to a boil and stir in 1 teaspoon salt. Add the leeks and cook for 7 minutes. Drain and place in a bowl of ice water to stop the cooking. Drain again and pat dry with paper towels. Place on a plate and let come to room temperature.

Warm a medium skillet over medium heat. Add the walnuts and rosemary. Cook, stirring occasionally, for 5 minutes, or until golden and fragrant. Coarsely chop.

In a small bowl, whisk together the oil, vinegar, and parsley. Season with salt and pepper.

Place the leeks on warmed serving plates, spoon the dressing over them, and sprinkle with the walnuts. Serve.

SMOKED TROUT SALAD A LA GRÈCQUE

Smoked trout is a good source of protein and omega-3 fatty acids. Packaged smoked trout is readily available and easy to keep on hand in the refrigerator to make this light salad.

SERVES 6

1	pound (450 g) smoked trout
5	small radishes, very thinly sliced
1	large English cucumber, peeled, seeded, and thinly sliced on the diagonal
1	celery rib, strings removed, thinly sliced on the diagonal
2	scallions, thinly sliced
24	red pear or cherry tomatoes, halved
$\frac{1}{2}$	cup pitted black olives
3	cups baby arugula leaves
$\frac{1}{4}$	cup (60 ml) extra-virgin olive oil
2	tablespoons (30 ml) red wine vinegar
1	teaspoon (5 ml) Dijon mustard
	Juice of $\frac{1}{2}$ lemon
	Kosher salt and freshly ground black pepper
$6\frac{1}{2}$	ounces (185 g) low-fat feta cheese, crumbled

Skin the trout and carefully remove the bones, keeping the flesh as intact as possible.

Place the radishes, cucumber, celery, scallions, tomatoes, olives, and arugula in a large salad bowl and gently toss to combine. Add the trout and gently toss; it will break into pieces.

In a small bowl, whisk together the oil, vinegar, mustard, and lemon juice. Season with salt and pepper and drizzle over the salad. Toss lightly. Divide among serving plates and sprinkle with the cheese. Serve.

Per serving: 310 calories, 22 g total fat, 6 g saturated fat, 26 g protein, 9 g carbohydrates, 2 g dietary fiber, 960 mg sodium

SPAGHETTI SQUASH SALAD

The flesh of spaghetti squash, when cooked, comes out like strands of cooked spaghetti and makes a light stand-in for pasta lovers. I often substitute it for pasta with my Tomato Sauce (page 170). For this spaghetti squash salad, take one more step and add nuts. Serve on its own or as "garden pasta" or with some shaved pecorino cheese.

SERVES 4

1	medium spaghetti squash
	Extra-virgin olive oil
	Kosher salt and freshly ground black pepper
½	cup hazelnuts
2	tablespoons (30 ml) hazelnut oil
2	tablespoons (30 ml) pure maple syrup (optional)

Per serving: 250 calories, 20 g total fat, 2 g saturated fat, 4 g protein, 18 g carbohydrates, 1 g dietary fiber, 70 mg sodium

Preheat the oven to 350°F (180°C). Cut the squash in half lengthwise and scoop out the seeds. Drizzle with olive oil and season with salt and pepper. Place, cut side down, in a large baking dish. Bake for 45 minutes, or until the strands may be loosened easily with a fork and the sides are soft when squeezed.

Put the hazelnuts in a medium skillet over low heat and toast until golden brown. Allow to cool. Place in a kitchen towel and rub to remove loose skins. Chop into large pieces.

Let the squash stand until cool enough to handle. Using a fork, scrape the squash strands into a large bowl. Add the hazelnuts and hazelnut oil, drizzle with the maple syrup, if using, and toss to serve.

SPAGHETTI SQUASH

I frequently use spaghetti squash in place of real spaghetti as an accompaniment to chicken, veal, or fish. It is terrific with tomato sauce.

THREE-BEAN CHILI WITH SOFT TACOS

Serve this crowd-pleaser with fresh guacamole, peeled and sliced jícama, and lots of lime wedges. It's especially good served the next day.

SERVES 6

1	tablespoon (15 ml) extra-virgin olive oil
1	medium onion, peeled and finely chopped
3	garlic cloves, peeled and minced
1	teaspoon ancho chile powder
1	teaspoon chili powder
1	teaspoon dried oregano, crushed
½	teaspoon ground cumin
1	can (28 ounces/800 g) unsalted stewed tomatoes, coarsely chopped
1	can (6 ounces/180 g) unsalted tomato paste
1	cup (240 ml) water
1	tablespoon (15 ml) Dijon mustard
1	can (15 ounces/450 g) red kidney beans, rinsed and drained (see note)
1	can (15 ounces/450 g) great Northern beans, rinsed and drained (see note)
1	can (15 ounces/450 g) chickpeas, rinsed and drained (see note)
2	medium carrots, peeled and chopped
2	small zucchini, chopped
1	cup fresh or frozen corn
	Hot pepper sauce
12	tortillas, warmed
	Guacamole (recipe follows)
	Jícama, peeled and sliced, for serving
	Lime wedges, for serving

Warm the oil in a large saucepan over medium heat. Add the onion and garlic; cook for 1 to 2 minutes. Stir in the ancho powder, chili powder, oregano, and cumin; cook for 1 minute. Stir in the tomatoes and their juice, tomato paste, water, and mustard.

Add the beans and chickpeas and bring to a boil. Reduce the heat, cover, and simmer for 15 minutes.

Stir in the carrots, zucchini, and corn. Cover and simmer for 10 minutes. Season with the pepper sauce.

Serve with warm tortillas and fresh guacamole and (if using) jícama and lime wedges.

NOTE: If using dried beans, soak ½ cup of each separately for 8 hours or overnight. Drain and rinse. Place the beans in a large saucepan and cover with water. Bring to a boil, then reduce the heat and simmer for 30 minutes. Drain and rinse, then continue with the recipe.

Per serving (with tortillas/no guacamole): 570 calories, 12 g total fat, 2.5 g saturated fat, 20 g protein, 102 g carbohydrates, 14 g dietary fiber, 1,080 mg sodium

GUACAMOLE

SERVES 4

2	ripe avocados
1	lemon, juiced
1	large onion, peeled and finely chopped
6	drops hot pepper sauce
4	drops Worcestershire sauce
9	cherry tomatoes, chopped

Scoop the flesh from the avocados into a medium bowl with the lemon juice, onion, hot pepper sauce and Worcestershire sauce. Mash coarsely together using a fork then stir in the cherry tomatoes. Gather the guacamole in the center of the bowl and cover, pressing the plastic wrap against the surface of the guaca-mole and refrigerate until serving.

Per serving: 190 calories, 16 g total fat, 2.5 g saturated fat, 3 g protein, 14 g carbohydrates, 6 g dietary fiber, 25 mg sodium

STEAMED TOFU

This tofu mixed with the pungent flavors of the dressing makes it anything but ordinary, and it is a great way to enjoy this nutritious food. Tofu is rich in protein, iron, and omega-3 fatty acids. Serve at lunch with steamed green vegetables, like asparagus and snap peas, and freshly cooked brown rice tossed with toasted flaked almonds and sesame seeds.

SERVES 4

DRESSING

- ⅓ cup (80 ml) Chinese black vinegar
- 3 tablespoons (45 ml) Chinese black soy sauce
- 3 tablespoons (45 ml) low-sodium soy sauce
- 2 tablespoons (30 ml) toasted sesame oil
- ¼ cup chopped scallions (white and green parts)
- ¼ cup chopped fresh cilantro
- 2 tablespoons peeled and finely diced fresh ginger
- ⅛ teaspoon crushed red pepper flakes

TOFU

- 1 package (14 ounces/400 g) organic silken tofu (see note)
- 1 tablespoon (15 ml) toasted sesame oil
- 1 tablespoon (15 ml) honey
  Juice of 2 limes
- 1 English cucumber, peeled, halved lengthwise, seeded, and julienned
- 1 medium zucchini, julienned
  Pinch of Szechuan pepper

For the dressing: In a small bowl, whisk together the vinegar, soy sauces, and oil. Stir in the scallions, cilantro, ginger, and pepper flakes.

For the tofu: Carefully invert the tofu onto a heat-proof serving plate and gently slice into even rectangular pieces. Place the plate in a steamer and steam for 10 minutes. Drain off any excess liquid.

In a small saucepan, combine the oil, honey, and lime juice. Stir over medium heat until very hot.

Spoon the dressing over the tofu, then pour the lime juice mixture over the tofu. Top with the cucumber and zucchini and sprinkle with the pepper before serving.

NOTE: Make sure to buy packaged tofu, as the kind sold in the open containers may harbor some bacteria.

Per serving: 240 calories, 14 g total fat, 1.5 g saturated fat, 12 g protein, 18 g carbohydrates, 2 g dietary fiber, 1,216 mg sodium

SICILIAN CAULIFLOWER WITH CAPERS

The lemon and capers add a Mediterranean flavor to the cauliflower, making it a good match with broiled fish and salad for a light meal.

SERVES 4 TO 6

1	teaspoon kosher salt, plus extra for seasoning
1	medium head cauliflower, cut into florets (about 4 cups)
¼	cup (60 ml) extra-virgin olive oil
2	tablespoons capers, rinsed and drained
	Juice of 1 lemon
	Freshly ground black pepper
1	lemon, cut into wedges

Bring a large pot of water to a boil. Stir in 1 teaspoon salt and add the cauliflower. Cook for 4 minutes, until al dente. Drain and transfer to paper towels; pat dry.

Heat the oil and capers in a large skillet over medium heat. Add the cauliflower and lemon juice. Cook, stirring occasionally, for 2 minutes, or until beginning to brown. Season with salt and pepper. Serve hot with lemon wedges.

Per serving (based on 4 servings): 170 calories, 14 g total fat, 2 g saturated fat, 3 g protein, 9 g carbohydrates, 3 g dietary fiber, 360 mg sodium

CUTTING A LEMON

Remember that fruit at room temperature gives more juice than chilled fruit. Before cutting the fruit, roll it firmly on a hard surface while pressing with your palm. This will help release even more juice. If you intend to zest the fruit, choose those with firm skin. Leaving lemon rind in any liquid imparts a bitter flavor.

To cut a lemon into wedges, wash it thoroughly and then trim the stem ends to the pith. Cut the lemon in half lengthwise and then in half again. If there is any pith remaining on the sides, remove it with a sharp knife. Remove any seeds.

To serve lemon halves for squeezing at the table, wash the fruit, cut it in half crosswise, and wrap each half with cheesecloth, securing the fabric with a ribbon or string.

PIZZA DOUGH

Making pizza from scratch allows experimentation with many different whole-grain flours that add not only nutrients but also flavor to the dough. I find that fresh, fragrant, and simple toppings make for the best pizzas.

MAKES 2 PIZZA SHELLS

4   cups unbleached all-purpose flour, plus extra for the counter (see note)

1   package active dry yeast

2   teaspoons salt

1   teaspoon sugar

1¼ cups (300 ml) warm water

1   tablespoon (15 ml) extra-virgin olive oil, plus extra for the bowl and plastic wrap

Per slice (based on 4 slices per pizza/no toppings):
250 calories, 2.5 g total fat, 0 g saturated fat, 7 g protein, 49 g carbohydrates, 2 g dietary fiber, 580 mg sodium

Mix the flour, yeast, salt, and sugar in a large bowl and make a well in the center. Pour the water and oil into the well and mix with a wooden spoon until most of the flour is incorporated. Use your hands to mix until a soft dough forms.

Turn the dough onto a floured counter and knead for 10 minutes. Put the kneaded dough into a lightly oiled bowl, brush the top with a little warm water, and cover with oiled plastic wrap. Set aside in a warm place until the dough doubles in size, about 40 minutes.

Punch down the dough and knead on a floured surface for 1 to 2 minutes. Divide in half and roll each half out to form a 6- by 12-inch (16 by 32 cm) rectangle about ¼ inch (6 mm) thick.

NOTE: If desired, replace half of the flour with whole-wheat or spelt flour.

RICOTTA AND FRESH HERB PIZZA

The delicate texture of the ricotta absorbs the flavors of the herbs and delivers a good balance of protein and calcium.

MAKES 2 PIZZAS

Pizza Dough (page 100)

2 cups chopped fresh herbs, such as parsley, chives, mint, and basil

Grated zest of 1 lemon

1 tablespoon peeled and finely chopped garlic

8 ounces (230 g) low-fat ricotta cheese

Extra-virgin olive oil

Kosher salt

Prepare the pizza dough.

Preheat the oven to 400°F (200°C). Mix the herbs, lemon zest, and garlic in a small bowl. Place each pizza shell on a baking sheet and spread evenly with the ricotta. Spoon on the herb mixture, drizzle with a little oil, and season with salt. Bake for 12 minutes, until the crust is golden.

Per slice (based on 4 slices per pizza): 280 calories, 4.5 g total fat, 1.5 g saturated fat, 10 g protein, 50 g carbohydrates, 2 g dietary fiber, 680 mg sodium

RICOTTA CHEESE

Just a few steps removed from fresh milk, cheeses such as ricotta, cottage cheese, and farmer cheese do not have the concentration of fat and sodium that hard cheeses do. They can be made from skim milk and are easy to find in low-fat and even fat-free versions. Part-skim ricotta, for instance, has about 40 percent less fat than the whole-milk cheese. And it packs a very respectable calcium punch: Ounce for ounce, ricotta has four times more calcium than the cottage cheese that it closely resembles. Ricotta is like a fine-textured cottage cheese and can be eaten by itself.

BEET PIZZA

This is an unusual topping for a pizza, but the combination of the thyme, Gruyère, and olives really intensifies the earthy aroma of the roasted beet root.

MAKES 2 PIZZAS

Pizza Dough (page 100)

8 ounces (230 g) low-fat mozzarella cheese, shredded

8 small beets, roasted, peeled, and thinly sliced or 1 recipe Balsamic Roast Beets (page 155)

4 ounces (115 g) Gruyère cheese, roughly chopped

6½ ounces (185 g) kalamata olives, pitted

½ cup fresh thyme leaves

Extra-virgin olive oil

Kosher salt and freshly ground black pepper

Prepare the pizza dough.

Preheat the oven to 400°F (200°C). Place each pizza shell on a baking sheet and sprinkle evenly with the mozzarella. Place the beet slices in rows across the pizzas. Scatter the Gruyère and olives over the beets. Sprinkle with the thyme, drizzle with oil, and season with salt and pepper. Bake for 15 minutes, until the crust is golden.

Per slice (based on 4 slices per pizza): 490 calories, 18 g total fat, 7 g saturated fat, 20 g protein, 60 g carbohydrates, 5 g dietary fiber, 1,230 mg sodium

GREEN PEA AND BEAN PUREE

Drizzle olive oil over this puree and serve warm as a dip with raw vegetables, or spread it on toast and top with fresh Boston lettuce and ripe tomatoes. If you don't have fresh peas, frozen peas retain not only their flavor but also their vitamin content.

SERVES 4

1	tablespoon (15 ml) extra-virgin olive oil
2	garlic cloves, peeled and crushed
1	cup shelled and peeled fresh fava beans
¼	cup (60 ml) water
2	tablespoons fresh tarragon
½	cup shelled fresh or frozen peas
1	cup canned white beans, rinsed and drained
	Kosher salt

Heat the oil in a large skillet over low heat. Add the garlic and cook for 1 minute. Stir in the fava beans and water. Simmer with the tarragon for 2 minutes. Add the peas and simmer for 1 minute, or until the favas are tender.

Transfer to a food processor and add the white beans. Puree, adding more water if necessary to give a smooth paste. Season with salt. Serve.

Per serving: 250 calories, 4.5 g total fat, 0.5 g saturated fat, 16 g protein, 39 g carbohydrates, 14 g dietary fiber, 330 mg sodium

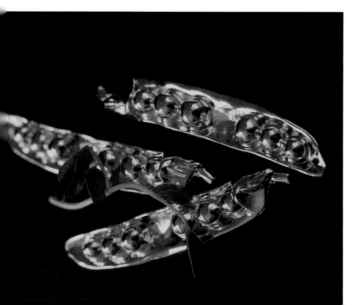

LEMON HUMMUS

Chickpeas (also called garbanzo beans) are rich in dietary fiber like most other beans. I like to serve this dip garnished with cucumber slices and pitted black olives, accompanied by fresh crudités.

SERVES 4

2	cups dried chickpeas
1	teaspoon grated lemon zest
	Juice of 4 lemons
6	garlic cloves, peeled
1	teaspoon (5 ml) extra-virgin olive oil
	Kosher salt and freshly ground black pepper

Per serving: 350 calories, 6 g total fat, 0 g saturated fat, 18 g protein, 60 g carbohydrates, 16 g dietary fiber, 50 mg sodium

Place the chickpeas in a bowl and add water to cover by 2 inches (5 cm). Soak overnight.

Drain and place the chickpeas in a large saucepan. Add water to cover by 2 inches (5 cm). Bring to a boil over high heat. Reduce the heat to medium-low and simmer gently for 1 hour, or until tender. Drain, reserving 1 cup (240 ml) of the cooking liquid.

Rinse the chickpeas with cold water and transfer to a blender. Add the lemon zest, lemon juice, garlic, and oil. Add enough of the reserved cooking liquid to cover the ingredients by 1 to 1½ inches (2.5 to 4 cm). Blend until the mixture is pureed and season with salt and pepper. Spoon the mixture into a bowl, cover, and refrigerate until needed.

WHOLE GRAINS

Whole grains contain antioxidants, lignans, phenolic acids, phytoestrogens, and other phytochemicals that may help reduce the risk of heart disease, cancer, and diabetes. But often the packaging on store-bought foods is confusing, and it is difficult to tell what is really whole grain. So read the labels carefully: If it says "100%" whole wheat, whole rye, or whole oats, that means it is made from whole grains. But "wheat flour" and "unbleached wheat flour" are not whole grain. Additionally, one can't rely on fiber numbers to choose whole grains. Breads, especially "light" loaves, may have added processed fiber, and they don't contain the same antioxidants and phytochemicals in true whole grains.

BROWN RICE WITH ORANGE

The difference between brown rice and white rice is not only color. Brown rice is the whole grain with only its inedible outer hull removed. White rice is further milled and polished, which removes the bran and the germ along with many of the nutrients. I always choose the healthier option of brown rice over white if it's available.

SERVES 4 TO 6

2	tablespoons (30 ml) extra-virgin olive oil
2	small onions, peeled and finely chopped
1½	cups long-grain brown rice
¼	teaspoon freshly ground black pepper
¼	teaspoon ground nutmeg
2½	cups (600 ml) vegetable broth
½	cup chopped fresh flat-leaf parsley
	Finely chopped zest and juice of 1 orange
½	cup chopped pistachio nuts (optional)

Heat the oil in a large saucepan over medium heat. Add the onions and cook, stirring, for 3 minutes, or until golden. Stir in the rice, pepper, and nutmeg. Add the broth and bring to a boil. Reduce the heat to low, cover, and cook for 40 minutes, or until tender.

Stir in the parsley and orange zest and juice. Transfer to a serving bowl. Sprinkle with the pistachios, if using.

Per serving (based on 4 servings): 370 calories, 10 g total fat, 1.5 g saturated fat, 7 g protein, 63 g carbohydrates, 4 g dietary fiber, 300 mg sodium

QUINOA PILAF

Quinoa is a recently rediscovered ancient "grain," native to Central America, where it was once known as the "Gold of the Incas" for its ability to sustain the strength of their warriors. It has a fluffy, creamy, slightly crunchy texture and a nutty flavor when cooked that is a good complement to the flavors in this pilaf.

SERVES 4 TO 6

1	cup quinoa
2	cups (480 ml) vegetable broth
1	bay leaf
1	tablespoon (15 ml) extra-virgin olive oil
1	teaspoon kosher salt
1/8	teaspoon freshly ground black pepper
1/2	teaspoon ground turmeric
1	tomato, finely chopped
1/2	red onion, peeled and finely chopped
1/2	cup pitted black olives (optional)
1/4	cup dried currants
1	teaspoon grated lemon zest
	Fresh mint leaves

Place the quinoa in a large sieve and rinse with cold water; drain. Transfer to a medium saucepan. Add the broth, bay leaf, oil, salt, pepper, and turmeric. Bring to a boil over medium heat, cover, and simmer for 15 to 20 minutes, or until the liquid is absorbed. Remove and discard the bay leaf.

Stir in the tomato, onion, olives (if using), currants, and lemon zest. Transfer to a serving dish and top with the mint.

Per serving (based on 4 servings): 250 calories, 6 g total fat, 1 g saturated fat, 7 g protein, 42 g carbohydrates, 4 g dietary fiber, 710 mg sodium

SALMON BURGERS

Recently I was a guest at a golf club where the chef cooked salmon burgers, served as you would meat burgers between toasted hamburger buns or an English muffin with lettuce, tomato, thinly sliced Vidalia onions, and red relish (which is similar to sweet red pepper relish). They were a delicious, light, and healthy alternative to a traditional burger.

SERVES 4

2	tablespoons (30 ml) extra-virgin olive oil
½	cup chopped scallions (white and green parts)
½	cup (120 ml) lemon juice
1	pound (450 g) skinless wild salmon fillets, bones removed, cut into 1-inch (2.5 cm) pieces
1	large egg, lightly beaten
2	tablespoons chopped fresh dill
¼	teaspoon freshly ground black pepper

Per serving: 260 calories, 15 g total fat, 2.5 g saturated fat, 25 g protein, 5 g carbohydrates, 0 g dietary fiber, 70 mg sodium

Heat 1 tablespoon (15 ml) of the oil in a medium nonstick skillet over medium heat. Add the scallions and cook for 2 minutes, or until translucent. Increase the heat to medium-high. Add the lemon juice and cook for 4 minutes, or until almost all the liquid evaporates. Transfer to a bowl to cool.

Place the raw salmon in a food processor and pulse until coarsely ground. Add to the scallions. Mix in the egg, dill, and pepper. Form into 4 equal patties.

Heat the remaining 1 tablespoon (15 ml) oil in a large nonstick skillet over medium-high heat. Sear the patties for about 2 minutes per side, or until golden brown and cooked through. Serve.

SOLE WITH TOASTED ALMONDS AND BANANAS

A combination that I imagined one evening, which has turned out to be quite successful. Leonard and I eat this every once in a while with a side dish of cooked long-grain rice mixed with raisins and served with cooked baby carrots and peas.

SERVES 4

½	cup sliced blanched almonds
4	sole fillets, 6 ounces (170 g) each
	Juice of 1 lemon
1	tablespoon (15 ml) extra-virgin olive oil
1	small onion, peeled and minced
2	garlic cloves, peeled and minced
2	small firm bananas, sliced

Per serving: 310 calories, 12 g total fat, 1.5 g saturated fat, 35 g protein, 15 g carbohydrates, 3 g dietary fiber, 140 mg sodium

Place the almonds in a small skillet and toast over medium heat for 5 minutes, or until golden. Set aside.

Place the fish on a plate and sprinkle with the lemon juice.

Heat the oil in a large nonstick skillet over low heat. Add the onion and garlic and cook until translucent, about 2 minutes.

Increase the heat to medium. Add the banana slices and fish (skin side up) to the skillet and cook until golden, about 4 minutes. Turn the pieces and cook for 1 minute, until the fish is opaque and the bananas have a crust.

Serve the fish and bananas sprinkled with the almonds.

BROCHETTES OF FISH

In our household, this is one of the most popular dishes that we make for the family. It is a simple way to have a casual meal, and it's delicious served with Brown Rice with Orange (page 105).

SERVES 4 TO 6

MARINADE

½	cup (120 ml) low-sodium soy sauce
1	cup fresh mint leaves, chopped
2	tablespoons (30 ml) honey
2	tablespoons (30 ml) extra-virgin olive oil
	Grated zest of 1 lime
	Juice of 4 limes
1	tablespoon peeled and grated fresh ginger
1	tablespoon coriander seeds, crushed
1	teaspoon pink peppercorns, crushed
	Kosher salt and freshly ground black pepper

For the marinade: In a small bowl, whisk together the soy sauce, mint, honey, oil, lime zest and juice, ginger, coriander, and peppercorns. Season with salt and pepper. Cover and set aside.

BROCHETTES

3	celery ribs, cut into 24 pieces
24	baby onions, peeled
2	large green bell peppers, cut into 1¼-inch (3 cm) square dice
24	small cremini mushrooms
24	red cherry tomatoes
12	sea scallops
12	medium shrimp, peeled and deveined
2	skinless salmon fillets, 6 ounces (170 g) each, cut into 1¼-inch (3 cm) pieces
2	skinless white fish fillets, such as halibut, 6 ounces (170 g) each, cut into 1¼-inch/3 cm pieces
	Lime wedges

Per serving (based on 4 servings): 450 calories, 12 g total fat, 2 g saturated fat, 52 g protein, 34 g carbohydrates, 5 g dietary fiber, 780 mg sodium

For the brochettes: Soak 12 bamboo skewers in water for 15 minutes.

Bring 2 inches (5 cm) of water to a simmer in a medium saucepan. Add the celery, onions, and peppers; cook for 5 minutes and then drain.

Alternately thread the vegetables and fish onto the skewers so each brochette each has 2 pieces of celery, 2 onions, 2 pieces of pepper, 2 mushrooms, 2 cherry tomatoes, 2 scallops, 2 shrimp, 1 piece of salmon, and 1 piece of white fish.

Pour the marinade into a large shallow dish and lay the brochettes in the marinade, turning to coat. Cover and refrigerate for 1 hour, turning the brochettes every 15 minutes.

Heat a large nonstick skillet over high heat or light a grill or broiler. Cook the brochettes for 5 minutes, turning once, until the shrimp are pink and the fish almost cooked through. At the same time, lightly cook the lime wedges. Serve the brochettes hot with the lime wedges on a bed of rice or quinoa.

TUNA WITH FENNEL, PISTACHIO, AND LEMON SPREAD

Tuna is firm and dense and has the meatiest flavor and texture of any fish. While canned tuna is a delicious and nutritious food, fresh tuna retains more of its beneficial omega-3 fats than canned.

SERVES 6

2	tablespoons (30 ml) plus 1 teaspoon (5 ml) extra-virgin olive oil
1	fennel bulb, thinly sliced
4	garlic cloves, peeled and thinly sliced
¼	cup (60 ml) water
¼	cup shelled pistachio nuts
	Grated zest of 1 lemon
	Juice of 2 lemons
6	tuna fillets, 5 ounces (145 g) each

Per serving: 250 calories, 9 g total fat, 1.5 g saturated fat, 35 g protein, 6 g carbohydrates, 2 g dietary fiber, 75 mg sodium

Heat 2 tablespoons (30 ml) of the oil in a large nonstick skillet over medium heat. Add the fennel and garlic; cook, stirring, for 2 minutes. As the fennel begins to caramelize, add the water and continue to cook for 3 minutes, until the fennel is tender and the water absorbed. Transfer to a food processor and add the pistachios and lemon zest and juice. Puree.

Wash the skillet and rub with the remaining 1 teaspoon (5 ml) oil. Add the tuna and cook over high heat for 2 minutes per side, keeping the center slightly rare. Remove to serving plates and serve with the fennel spread.

BAKED MARINATED CHICKEN

Though the chicken is cooked in the oven, this marinade gives it a barbecued flavor that is always popular, especially with children.

SERVES 6

12	skinless chicken drumsticks or thighs or 24 wing drumettes
1	cup (240 ml) red wine
$2/3$	cup (160 ml) low-sodium soy sauce
$1/3$	cup (80 ml) honey
1	medium onion, peeled and finely chopped
2	garlic cloves, peeled and minced
1	tablespoon peeled and grated fresh ginger

Place the chicken in a single layer in a large ovenproof dish. In a medium bowl, mix the wine, soy sauce, honey, onion, garlic, and ginger. Pour over the chicken pieces, cover, and refrigerate overnight.

Preheat the oven to 350°F (180°C). Uncover the chicken and bake, basting frequently, for 1 hour, or until a glaze forms. Serve warm.

Per serving: 260 calories, 4.5 g total fat, 1 g saturated fat, 27 g protein, 21 g carbohydrates, 0 g dietary fiber, 1,060 mg sodium

STUFFED RED PEPPERS

Colorful bell peppers are an excellent source of vitamin C
and other antioxidants. I like to use a mix of red, yellow,
orange, and green peppers when I'm making this for a
group. Choose peppers with straight sides and even bases
so they'll stand up properly. Serve with Tomato Sauce (page
170) ladled around the base of the peppers.

SERVES 6

STUFFED PEPPERS

6	small to medium red peppers

FILLING

1	tablespoon (15 ml) extra-virgin olive oil
1	medium onion, peeled and finely chopped
1	celery rib, finely chopped
2	garlic cloves, peeled and finely chopped
8	ounces (230 g) ground white meat of chicken or turkey
1½	cups cooked long-grain brown or white rice
¼	cup pine nuts (optional)
2	tablespoons finely chopped fresh flat-leaf parsley
	Kosher salt and freshly ground black pepper

Per serving: 260 calories, 4 g total fat, 0.5 g saturated
fat, 1 g protein, 43 g carbohydrates, 4 g dietary fiber,
55 mg sodium

Preheat the oven to 350°F (180°C).

For the peppers: Cut the stem end from the
peppers and reserve, keeping matching tops and
bases together. Remove the seeds and mem-
branes from the peppers with a grapefruit knife.

For the filling: Warm the oil in a large skillet over
medium heat. Add the onion, celery, and garlic;
cook for 5 minutes, or until soft. Add the chicken
or turkey and cook, stirring occasionally, for 5
minutes, or until just cooked. Remove from the
heat and stir in the rice, pine nuts (if using), and
parsley. Season with salt and pepper.

Spoon the filling into the peppers, leaving about
½ inch (1.3 cm) at the top, and replace the tops.
Fit the peppers close together into a casserole
dish just large enough to hold them. Cover and
bake for 45 minutes, or until the peppers are
tender.

OVEN-POACHED LEMON CHICKEN

Poached as a whole bird, this chicken is very tender. It would be perfect served with the Green Pea and Bean Puree (page 103) and Coleslaw (page 83).

SERVES 4 TO 6

1	chicken, about 4 pounds (2 kg)
1	small red onion, peeled
1	small lemon, thinly sliced
6	bay leaves
3	fresh lemon thyme sprigs
2	garlic cloves, peeled

Per serving (without skin, based on 4 servings):
320 calories, 9 g total fat, 2.5 g saturated fat,
55 g protein, 0 g carbohydrates, 0 g dietary fiber,
150 mg sodium

Preheat the oven to 325°F (160°C). Rinse the chicken inside and out with cold water and pat dry. Insert the onion into the cavity. Lift the skin on either side of the breast bone and slide the lemon slices and 4 of the bay leaves under the skin.

Place the chicken in an ovenproof casserole. Add enough cold water to reach just under the shoulder joints, being careful no water enters the cavity. Add the remaining 2 bay leaves, lemon thyme, and garlic to the water. Cover and bake for 1 to 1½ hours, or until an instant-read thermometer inserted into the lower meaty part of the thigh registers 170°F (75°C). Remove the chicken from the oven and let rest for 10 minutes before serving.

To serve, carve the chicken, discarding the bay leaves, and transfer to warmed plates or allow to cool and pull the meat from the bones. Although you may want to leave the skin on for the presentation, I don't recommend eating the skin as it is high in fat and calories.

TURKEY PAILLARD

Paillard is the culinary term for a thin slice of meat. Ask your butcher to slice it very thin, or if you're slicing it yourself, freezing the meat before you do so makes it easier. Since turkey contains tryptophan, it is believed to be an aid in sleeping well.

SERVES 6

1	boneless, skinless turkey breast, about 1½ pounds (680 g)
	Kosher salt and freshly cracked black pepper
2	tablespoons fresh thyme leaves, finely chopped
6	fresh sage leaves, finely chopped
1	tablespoon (15 ml) extra-virgin olive oil
6	ripe tomatoes, chopped
1	large bunch arugula, chopped (about 4 cups)
6	teaspoons (30 ml) balsamic vinegar

Per serving: 190 calories, 3.5 g total fat, 0.5 g saturated fat, 29 g protein, 8 g carbohydrates, 2 g dietary fiber, 90 mg sodium

Preheat the oven to 375°F (190°C).

Slice the turkey on the bias into six ½-inch (1.3 cm) slices. Season with salt, if desired, and pepper and rub with the thyme and sage.

Heat the oil in a large ovenproof skillet over high heat. Sauté the turkey slices for 2 minutes per side, or until golden. Transfer to the oven and bake for 5 minutes, until the meat is cooked through. Transfer the turkey to individual plates. To serve, top each plate with a portion of the tomatoes and arugula and drizzle with 1 teaspoon (5 ml) vinegar.

MOROCCAN MEATBALLS

These meatballs are made with chickpeas (also called garbanzo beans), which is a good way to include more fiber and nutrients when making recipes that use ground meat. Serve with Tomato Sauce (page 170) for classic fare or place a few meatballs each on a bamboo skewer and serve with Lemon Hummus (page 104) and a salad. Traditionally, the meat is wrapped around a stainless steel skewer in a marquis shape and baked in the oven.

SERVES 4 TO 6

Extra-virgin olive oil

1	pound (450 g) lean ground beef
1	cup canned chickpeas, rinsed and finely chopped
1/2	cup pine nuts
1	large egg
1	onion, peeled and minced
1/4	cup minced fresh flat-leaf parsley
2	garlic cloves, peeled and minced
1	teaspoon ground cumin

Kosher salt and freshly ground black pepper

Preheat the oven to 350°F (180°C). Grease a baking dish with the oil.

In a large bowl, mix the beef, chickpeas, pine nuts, egg, onion, parsley, and garlic. Add the cumin and season with salt and pepper; mix again. Shape into small meatballs, about 1 inch (2.5 cm) round, and place in the baking dish. Bake for 35 minutes, or until cooked through.

Per serving (based on 4 servings): 360 calories, 20 g total fat, 3.5 g saturated fat, 29 g protein, 20 g carbohydrates, 4 g dietary fiber, 290 mg sodium

NOISETTES OF LAMB WITH LEMON

By using trim lamb noisettes, you avoid the fat on many other cuts of lamb. They would make a wonderful casual lunch served with the Fava and Edamame Salad with Toasted Almonds (page 152) or more of a meal with the Sweet and Sour Red Cabbage (page 156).

SERVES 4

Grated zest of 1 lemon

Juice of 2 lemons

2   large garlic cloves, peeled and crushed

1   tablespoon (15 ml) extra-virgin olive oil

8   lamb noisettes, about 1 inch (2.5 cm) thick

Freshly ground black pepper

$\frac{1}{8}$ teaspoon ground nutmeg

2   tablespoons fresh thyme leaves

Per serving: 200 calories, 10 g total fat, 3 g saturated fat, 24 g protein, 3 g carbohydrates, 0 g dietary fiber, 80 mg sodium

In a shallow glass dish, combine the lemon zest, lemon juice, garlic, and oil. Add the lamb and turn to coat. Cover and marinate for 30 minutes, turning once.

Place a large cast-iron skillet over medium-high and heat until hot. Sprinkle the lamb with pepper and nutmeg. Reserving the marinade, transfer the lamb to the skillet and cook for 6 minutes, turning once. Transfer to serving plates.

Add a little water to the reserved marinade, pour into the skillet, and bring to a boil. Deglaze the pan by scraping up the browned bits on the bottom into the sauce. Stir in the thyme and spoon over the lamb.

THYME AND HONEY ROAST PORK WITH BEANS

Baked in the oven, this pork loin is wonderful combined with the fresh fava beans, making it a light meat dish full of flavor.

SERVES 6

6	fresh thyme sprigs
1	pork loin (2.3 pounds/1 kg), keeping ribs, skin and fat removed, tied with string
	Extra-virgin olive oil
3	strips orange zest
¾	cup (180 ml) white wine
¼	cup (60 ml) honey
	Kosher salt and freshly ground black pepper
1	cup (240 ml) warm water
7	ounces (200 g) shallots, peeled and chopped
4	garlic cloves, peeled and chopped
3	cups shelled fresh fava beans, cooked and peeled
1	cup canned cannellini beans, rinsed and drained
¼	cup dried currants
4	fresh sage leaves

Per serving: 420 calories, 10 g total fat, 3.5 g saturated fat, 40 g protein, 38 g carbohydrates, 5 g dietary fiber, 430 mg sodium

Preheat the oven to 350°F (180°C).

Tuck the thyme sprigs under the string around the pork. Rub the pork with a little oil and place in a baking dish with the orange zest. Mix the wine and honey and pour over the pork. Season with salt and pepper.

Roast for 1 to 1¼ hours, or when the meat registers 170°F (75°C), for well done when tested with a meat thermometer, basting occasionally. Transfer the pork to a serving platter and cover to keep warm.

Let the baking dish cool for a few minutes. Pour the water into the dish and deglaze, stirring to incorporate the browned bits.

Heat 1 teaspoon (5 ml) oil in a large skillet and cook the shallots and garlic until soft. Add the fava and cannellini beans, currants, sage, and the juices from the baking dish. Season with salt and pepper. Simmer for 10 to 15 minutes, adding more water if the mixture becomes too dry. Slice the pork into individual ribs and serve with the beans.

STEAMED ASPARAGUS
WITH BASIC AIOLI

When asparagus is in season, nothing is simpler or more elegant as a starter than a plate of perfectly steamed asparagus with a garlicky aioli sauce.

SERVES 8 AS AN APPETIZER

2   large bunches asparagus, about
     2–2½ pounds (0.9–1.2 kg)

Per serving (with aioli): 260 calories, 29 g total fat, 4.5 g saturated fat, 3 g protein, 5 g carbohydrates, 2 g dietary fiber, 340 mg sodium

Rinse the asparagus and remove the ends by snapping where they break naturally. Trim the buds from the stalk using a sharp knife. Add 1 inch (2.5 cm) of water to the bottom of a large saucepan and bring to a simmer over medium heat. Place the asparagus in a steamer basket, cover, and steam for 5 to 6 minutes, or until tender but green. Serve with basic aioli.

BASIC AIOLI

MAKES 1 CUP (240 ML)

4	garlic cloves, peeled and finely chopped
1	teaspoon salt
2	tablespoons (30 ml) Dijon mustard
2	large egg yolks
1	cup (240 ml) extra-virgin olive oil
1	tablespoon (15 ml) warm water
4	teaspoons (20 ml) lemon juice

Place the garlic and salt in a mortar and grind slowly with the pestle, moving in one direction only. (You can do this step in a food processor if you'd like.) Transfer the garlic to a medium bowl. Whisk in the mustard and then the egg yolks.

Very slowly dribble in ½ cup (120 ml) of the oil while whisking the mixture. (This must be done very slowly or the oil will not emulsify and your sauce will not thicken.) Whisk in the water and lemon juice. Then slowly whisk in the remaining ½ cup (120 ml) oil. The mixture will thicken as you continue to blend it. The mixture should be slightly thinner than commercial mayonnaise. If it becomes too thick, you can add a bit more warm water, 1 teaspoon (5 ml) at a time.

TRIMMING ASPARAGUS

Freshly harvested asparagus spears need to be kept in cool, humid conditions. Cut a little off the bottom, stand them upright in a deep container with ½ inch (1 cm) of cold water, and store them in the refrigerator.

To clean the spears, mix a little salt with some warm water and gently swish the asparagus around in the mixture to remove any sand. Rinse and drain on paper towels.

It's best to trim asparagus by breaking off the thick end of each spear. It will naturally break at the spot where it is tender. Cutting the ends off with a knife might leave you with unpleasant woody stems.

Lay the trimmed asparagus spears on a board. Trim the small triangular "buds" from the stalks using a knife. Then use a vegetable peeler to lightly scrape the length of each stalk just below the leaf buds to the trimmed end. A pale hint of green should be left on the asparagus.

Steaming the asparagus in an upright basket allows the ends to cook and the spears to remain al dente.

CLOCKWISE FROM TOP: SIMPLE VINAIGRETTE (PAGE 148), BASIC AIOLI (PAGE 123), CRANBERRY RELISH (PAGE 194), AVOCADO WATERCRESS COULIS (PAGE 71) AND MANGO SALSA (OPPOSITE PAGE)

MANGO SALSA

This recipe is a "killer." We use it for salmon, but it would be as good with chicken. It can be made a day in advance since it is best served chilled.

SERVES 4 TO 6

1	Bermuda onion, peeled and finely chopped
$\frac{1}{2}$	red bell pepper, finely diced
$\frac{1}{2}$	green bell pepper, finely diced
$\frac{1}{2}$	yellow bell pepper, finely diced
1	pint red cherry tomatoes, quartered
2	firm, ripe mangoes, peeled and diced
$\frac{1}{2}$	teaspoon sugar
	Juice of 1 lemon
1	cup roughly chopped cilantro leaves

In a medium bowl, mix together the onion, peppers, tomatoes, and mangoes. Stir the sugar into the lemon juice and pour over the salsa; stir to combine. Add the cilantro and gently toss to combine. Cover and refrigerate until needed.

Per serving (based on 4 servings): 110 calories, 0.5 g total fat, 0 g saturated fat, 2 g protein, 28 g carbohydrates, 4 g dietary fiber, 15 mg sodium

CHEESECAKE WITH CHOCOLATE COOKIE CRUST

Many years ago, I saw a recipe for cheesecake in *Gourmet* magazine that looked terrific but was very decadent. I wondered if I could get the same result using fat-free ingredients, and although it took several attempts, I think I've perfected the recipe. We did a comparison tasting, and all have declared the fat-free recipe tasted richer! I often make this on the Fourth of July as part of a red, white, and blue dessert buffet, then I arrange red raspberries in a star pattern on a field of blueberries on the top of the cheesecake.

SERVES 8 TO 10

CRUST

36	chocolate wafer cookies
½	cup (115 g) unsalted butter, melted

FILLING

32	ounces (920 g) fat-free cream cheese, at room temperature
⅔	cup sugar
2	tablespoons unbleached all-purpose flour
4	large eggs
½	cup (115 g) fat-free sour cream
1½	teaspoons (7 ml) vanilla extract
1	teaspoon grated orange zest
1	teaspoon grated lemon zest
½	teaspoon salt
	Mixed berries and fruit, for topping

For the crust: Grind the cookies in a food processor to form fine crumbs (about 1½ cups). Transfer to a bowl and stir in the butter. Press the mixture firmly into the bottom and ½ inch (1.3 cm) up the sides of a 9½-inch (23.3 cm) nonstick springform pan. Refrigerate for 30 minutes.

For the filling: Preheat the oven to 325°F (160°C).

Place the cream cheese in a medium bowl and beat with a hand-held electric mixer until light and fluffy. Gradually beat in the sugar and then the flour. Beat in the eggs, one at a time. Beat in the sour cream, vanilla extract, orange and lemon zests, and salt until well combined.

Remove the crust from the refrigerator and pour in the cheese filling. Bake the cheesecake on a foil-lined shallow baking pan in the middle of the

oven for 1 hour and 10 minutes. (The cheesecake will not be completely set; it sets as it cools.) Turn off the oven, prop the door open about 6 inches (15 cm), and allow the cheesecake to stand in the oven until completely cooled. Cover and refrigerate overnight.

To serve, remove the side of the pan and arrange berries and fruit to cover the top of the cake.

Per serving (based on 8 servings): 400 calories, 19 g total fat, 10 g saturated fat, 23 g protein, 35 g carbohydrates, 2 g dietary fiber, 970 mg sodium

BLACK RICE PUDDING WITH BANANA "ICE CREAM"

Black or "forbidden" rice is black-colored rice that turns purple upon cooking. It has a sweet taste and sticky texture and all the nutritional benefits of whole-grain rice. Paired with a fruit "ice cream," this dessert is an unusual but healthful sweet.

SERVES 4 TO 6

1	cup Thai black sticky rice or forbidden rice
2	cups (480 ml) unsweetened pear juice
2	cups (480 ml) cold water
	Banana "Ice Cream" (recipe follows)

Per serving (based on 4 servings with "ice cream"):
270 calories, 1 g total fat, 0 g saturated fat, 3 g protein, 64 g carbohydrates, 3 g dietary fiber, 5 mg sodium

Place the rice in a sieve and rinse with cold water. Transfer to a bowl and add enough cold water to cover the rice by at least 1 inch (2.5 cm). Let stand in a cool place for 8 hours or overnight. Drain.

In a heavy saucepan, combine the rice, pear juice, and 2 cups water. Bring to a boil over high heat. Reduce the heat to medium-low, cover, and simmer gently for $1\frac{1}{2}$ to $1\frac{3}{4}$ hours, until all the liquid is absorbed and the rice is tender but still maintains a little texture. Be sure to stir occasionally to prevent any scorching or sticking on the bottom of the pan. If the rice looks as though it's becoming too dry, add a little more water. The texture of the pudding should be very thick. Remove the pan from the heat and cool.

Spoon the rice pudding into individual bowls and serve with the "ice cream."

BANANA "ICE CREAM"

This frozen treat is so easy to make and can be varied to use any favorite fruit.

SERVES 4

4 ripe bananas
Pinch of ground nutmeg
Pinch of ground cinnamon

Peel the bananas, break into large sections, and place in a large resealable plastic bag. Freeze until solid, at least 2 hours or overnight.

About 2 hours before serving, place the frozen bananas in a food processor and process until pureed. Stir in the nutmeg and cinnamon. Transfer to a metal container (a bowl or even a cake pan will do) and return to the freezer until firm, about 2 hours.

About 10 minutes before serving, remove from the freezer. Serve with the rice pudding.

FRUIT CLAFOUTI

This is a favorite of my daughter-in-law Karen and has stood the test of time to many rave reviews. You can choose one fruit or make a medley of whatever is in season.

SERVES 6

Butter for baking dish

1 tablespoon (15 ml) mild-flavored honey

2 tablespoons (30 ml) Kirsh or fruit liqueur (my favorite is Amaretto), optional

4 large egg whites

2 large egg yolks

1/4 cup plus 2 tablespoons sugar

1 teaspoon (5 ml) vanilla extract

1/2 teaspoon (2 ml) almond extract

1 cup sifted unbleached flour

1 1/2 cups (340 g) fat-free plain yogurt

Pinch of salt

4 cups fruit, such as strawberries, blackberries, blueberries, pitted cherries, or sliced peaches, or plums

2 teaspoons chopped dried apricots, soaked in water to soften

2 teaspoons confectioners' sugar for dusting (optional)

Per serving: 70 calories, 0.5 g total fat, 0 g saturated fat, 1 g protein, 15 g carbohydrates, 5 g dietary fiber, 0 mg sodium

Preheat the oven to 400°F (200°C). Lightly butter an oval 6-cup (1.5-liter) ovenproof dish.

In the bowl of an electric mixer, beat together the honey, liqueur (if using), egg whites, egg yolks, sugar, vanilla extract, and almond extract. Slowly beat in the flour, then add the yogurt and salt and mix together well, but gently.

Spread the fruit and the softened apricots in the baking dish. Pour the batter over the fruit and place on the upper rack of the oven. Bake for 30 to 40 minutes, until golden. Place a doily over the top of the dish and sprinkle with confectioners' sugar to decorate, if using.

VARIATIONS

Sprinkle 1/2 cup sliced almonds over the clafouti after it has been in the oven for 15 minutes.

Apricot Sauce: Chop 6 dried apricots and soak them in 1 cup (240 ml) water for 1 hour; puree to serve as a fruit sauce over the clafouti.

ALMOND MILK BLANCMANGE WITH POACHED PEACHES

These delicate molded desserts are an interesting alternative to custard and offer the health benefits of the almond milk, which is high in calcium and a good milk alternative for people who are lactose intolerant.

SERVES 4

BLANCMANGE

3	cups blanched almonds
4	cups (1 liter) hot water
2	tablespoons (30 ml) cold water
1	tablespoon (15 ml) unflavored gelatin
¼	cup sugar

PEACHES

2	cups (480 ml) white grape juice
	Juice of 1 lemon
1	lemon, sliced
2	tablespoons (30 ml) honey
½	teaspoon ground cinnamon
3	cloves
3	firm, ripe peaches, cut into quarters, seeds removed

Per serving: 210 calories, 3.5 g total fat, 0 g saturated fat, 5 g protein, 43 g carbohydrates, 2 g dietary fiber, 160 mg sodium

For the blancmange: Combine the almonds and 3 cups (720 ml) of the hot water in a food processor; blend to a fine paste. Working in batches, press the almond mixture through a fine sieve set over a large saucepan. Return the paste to the food processor with the remaining 1 cup (240 ml) hot water and pulse again to extract as much "almond milk" as possible. Strain into the saucepan. Discard the solids.

In a custard cup, sprinkle the gelatin over the cold water. Let stand for 2 minutes to soften.

Add the sugar to the saucepan and stir over medium heat until dissolved. Heat until almost boiling, then remove from the heat and stir in the gelatin until dissolved. Pour into a 2½-cup (600 ml) mold or individual ramekins. Cover and refrigerate until set, 5 hours or overnight.

For the peaches: In a large saucepan, combine the grape juice, lemon juice, lemon slices, honey, cinnamon, and cloves; bring to a boil over high heat. Reduce the heat to medium-low, add the peaches, and poach gently until tender and richly colored, about 30 minutes. Let cool, then serve the peaches and syrup with the blancmange.

BERRIES MARINATED IN BALSAMIC VINEGAR

This dessert is simple, refreshing, and bursting with antioxidants. Serve as is or with a drizzle of low-fat vanilla yogurt or a scoop of your favorite sorbet.

SERVES 4

½   cup (120 ml) balsamic vinegar
3   tablespoons brown sugar
1   tablespoon (15 ml) vanilla extract
1   cup sliced strawberries
1   cup blackberries
1   cup raspberries

In a small bowl, whisk together the vinegar, brown sugar, and vanilla extract. Place the berries in a large bowl and pour the vinegar mixture over them. Toss lightly to combine. Let the fruit marinate for 15 to 20 minutes. Drain. Serve immediately or cover and chill.

Per serving: 70 calories, 0.5 g total fat, 0 g saturated fat, 1 g protein, 15 g carbohydrates, 5 g dietary fiber, 0 mg sodium

NIGHT

EVELINDA COCKTAIL

I did not include many alcoholic drinks in this book, but this one is so special that I felt I couldn't leave it out. The Evelinda was created for me by my friend Ellery Gordon, who is a great cook, and it contains Mandarine Napoléon, a cognac-based liqueur flavored with Sicilian tangerines. If you can't find Mandarine Napoléon, substitute Cointreau or Triple Sec.

SERVES 20

1	pint kumquats
¾	cup (180 ml) honey
¾	cup (180 ml) water
	Grated zest of 1 orange
	Grated zest of 1 lemon
¼	cup (60 ml) Mandarine Napoléon, Cointreau, or Triple Sec
4	bottles champagne

Per serving: 180 calories, 0 g total fat, 0 g saturated fat, 0 g protein, 37 g carbohydrates, 2 g dietary fiber, 0 mg sodium

Trim the stem ends of the kumquats and slice into ⅛-inch (3 mm) rings, removing the seeds. Place in a heavy nonreactive saucepan with the honey, water, orange zest, and lemon zest; stir to combine. Cook over medium-low heat, stirring occasionally, until the kumquats have a glossy, smooth appearance, about 8 to 10 minutes.

Drain the kumquats, reserving the syrup, and place the kumquats in a glass bowl. Return the syrup to the pan and cook over low heat until the syrup thickens, about 10 minutes. Allow to cool. Pour the syrup over the kumquats and stir in the Mandarine Napoléon. Cover and refrigerate for at least 2 hours or overnight.

To prepare an Evelinda, place 3 or 4 kumquat slices and ½ teaspoon (2 ml) of the liquid in a champagne flute. Fill with champagne.

Store the leftover kumquat mixture in a sealed jar in the refrigerator for up to 2 weeks.

BABY BELLINI

A glass of champagne is a grown-up way to celebrate very special occasions, but this Bellini will delight both the young and young at heart. Serve in a pitcher at a weekend brunch gathering.

SERVES 2

½	cup (120 ml) peach nectar
¼	cup (60 ml) lemon juice
1½	cups (360 ml) sparkling apple juice

Mix the peach nectar and lemon juice and divide between 2 champagne flutes. Top off each glass with apple juice. Serve.

Per serving: 130 calories, 0 g total fat, 0 g saturated fat, 0 g protein, 33 g carbohydrates, 0 g dietary fiber, 10 mg sodium

SPICED POMEGRANATE SPARKLER

Pomegranates contain polyphenol, a powerful antioxidant. Pomegranate juice is widely available, but I like to buy whole fruit, squeezing the chilled halves as you would oranges in fall and winter and sprinkling the seeds on salads.

SERVES 2

½   cup (120 ml) unsweetened cranberry juice
3   cinnamon sticks
1   star anise
1   cup (240 ml) pomegranate juice
1   cup (240 ml) sparkling water
     Ice cubes
2   lime wedges

Bring the cranberry juice to a simmer in a small saucepan over medium heat; add 1 cinnamon stick and the star anise. Simmer for 10 minutes. Remove from the heat and let cool. Discard the cinnamon stick and star anise.

Stir in the pomegranate juice and sparkling water. Pour over ice and garnish with lime wedges and the remaining 2 cinnamon sticks. Serve.

Per serving: 140 calories, 0 g total fat, 0 g saturated fat, 0 g protein, 35 g carbohydrates, 1 g dietary fiber, 20 mg sodium

BASIC VEGETABLE STOCK

It's a good idea to make batches of stock and freeze them in 2-cup (480 ml) containers. A spice sachet adds flavor to almost any soup or stew.

MAKES ABOUT 3 QUARTS (3 LITERS)

1	parsnip
2	leeks, cleaned and chopped
4	yellow onions, peeled and chopped
6	celery ribs, chopped
6	carrots, peeled and chopped
1	garlic head, cut in half
1	spice sachet (see note)
13	cups (3 liters) cold water

Per cup: 20 calories, 0 g total fat, 0 g saturated fat, 1 g protein, 5 g carbohydrates, 0 g dietary fiber, 25 mg sodium

Place the vegetables in a large pot with the spice sachet. Cover with the water and bring to a boil. Simmer uncovered at a lazy bubble for 2 to 3 hours; skim away any scum that rises to the surface but do not stir. Pour through a strainer lined with dampened cheesecloth, return to the pot, and cook over medium-high heat for an additional hour to reduce and concentrate the flavors.

NOTE: To make a spice sachet, take a square of cheesecloth and wrap 6 cracked peppercorns, 4 parsley stems, 1 thyme sprig, and 1 bay leaf in it. Twist the ends of the cloth together and tie with cooking string. When adding to the pot, tie one end to the handle for easy removal. A basic sachet will flavor 3 quarts (3 liters) of liquid.

WATER

I always use bottled or purified water in my tea, coffee, and recipes, especially when making soups and sauces. Since the mineral content of water varies so much from place to place, using bottled water ensures that there will be less chance of the taste of food being affected by the these minerals.

BROCCOLI SOUP

Puréed soups are a big hit in our house; I like them thick, as they are very flavorful that way. A simple vegetable stock is the base for them all, and then I buy the freshest vegetables in stores to create many different varieties.

SERVES 4

1	tablespoon (15 ml) extra-virgin olive oil
1	leek, cleaned and thinly sliced
1	garlic clove, peeled and minced
1	medium onion, peeled and finely chopped
2	medium potatoes, peeled and finely chopped
1	pound (450 g) broccoli, flowers and peeled stems, chopped into 1-inch (2.5 cm) chunks
5	cups (1.2 liters) Basic Vegetable Stock (page 139)
	Kosher salt and freshly ground black pepper
	Ground nutmeg

Heat the oil in a large saucepan over medium heat. Add the leek, garlic, and onion; cook, stirring, until the onion is translucent. Add the potatoes, broccoli, and stock; bring to a simmer. Cook for 20 minutes, or until the vegetables are tender.

Using a blender or food processor, puree the soup in batches. Return to the pot and season with salt, pepper, and nutmeg. Simmer for 10 minutes before serving.

VARIATIONS
Replace the broccoli with 1 pound (450 g) of asparagus (ends trimmed), frozen peas, celery, butternut squash (peeled and chopped), carrots, or any vegetable.

Per serving: 190 calories, 4 g total fat, 0.5 g saturated fat, 6 g protein, 36 g carbohydrates, 7 g dietary fiber, 105 mg sodium

SOUP CONDIMENTS
Soups are a matter of taste, and a simple condiment can change the mood to suit. Leonard and I really enjoy broccoli, pea, or asparagus soup served with a dollop of yogurt and a sprinkle of curry.

Try mixing some grated fresh ginger into squash or carrot soup, or make mixes of ground spices like cardamom and chili to sprinkle over freshly made soups. You can also chop fresh herbs and mix them with chopped heated seeds and nuts for great garnishes: Try rosemary and pumpkin seeds or thyme and pine nuts.

CIOPPINO

On Leonard's and my first trip to Vancouver, we found a lovely restaurant that served up a cioppino made from the freshest catch of the day. When I make my version of this soup, it always brings back memories of the trip.

SERVES 4 TO 6

1	tablespoon fennel seeds
	Grated zest of 1 orange
	Kosher salt and freshly ground black pepper
2	tablespoons (30 ml) extra-virgin olive oil
8	ounces (230 g) halibut or other firm white fish, skin removed, cut into chunks
8	ounces (230 g) salmon, skin removed, cut into chunks
8	ounces (230 g) medium shrimp, peeled and deveined
8	ounces (230 g) scallops
3	large garlic cloves, peeled and chopped
1	teaspoon minced fresh rosemary
1/4	teaspoon red pepper flakes
1	can (28 ounces/800 g) crushed Italian tomatoes
1	bay leaf
1	cup (240 ml) fish stock or dry white wine
	Pinch of sugar
	Hot water
2	tablespoons minced fresh flat-leaf parsley
2	tablespoons chopped chives
2	tablespoons chopped fresh dill

Using a mortar and pestle, crush together the fennel seeds, orange zest, a pinch of salt, a generous grind of pepper, and 1 tablespoon (15 ml) of the oil. Place the fish, shrimp, and scallops in a glass bowl and combine with the fennel mixture. Cover and refrigerate for 1 hour to marinate.

Heat the remaining 1 tablespoon (15 ml) oil in a large pot over low heat. Add the garlic, rosemary, and pepper flakes; cook for 1 to 2 minutes, or until fragrant. Increase the heat, add the tomatoes with their juice and the bay leaf, and bring to a simmer. Cook until the tomatoes begin to break down and thicken, about 20 minutes, then reduce the heat to low.

Add the stock and sugar; simmer gently until reduced, about 15 minutes. Add the marinated seafood and enough hot water just to cover; stir gently to combine. Bring the soup to a boil and remove from the heat as soon as the fish pieces become opaque, about 5 minutes. Stir in the parsley, chives, and dill and serve immediately.

Per serving (based on 4 servings): 420 calories, 17 g total fat, 3 g saturated fat, 48 g protein, 19 g carbohydrates, 5 g dietary fiber, 730 mg sodium

CHICKEN SOUP

Every household should have a good basic recipe for chicken soup. Treating a cold or fever with chicken soup is an ancient and time-honored home remedy. If nothing else, a bowl of soup, lovingly prepared, can make us think we feel better. The trick for my version is the addition of dill and parsnip, which give it a wonderful flavor.

SERVES 6

1	small pullet chicken (see note)
1	tablespoon kosher salt
3	large parsnips, coarsely chopped
2	large carrots, peeled and coarsely chopped
2	celery ribs, coarsely chopped
1	bunch fresh dill
½	bunch fresh flat-leaf parsley sprigs
8	cups (2 liters) water
¼	cup minced fresh flat-leaf parsley

Per serving: 190 calories, 12 g total fat, 3.5 g saturated fat, 15 g protein, 6 g carbohydrates, 1 g dietary fiber, 450 mg sodium

Place the chicken in a large dish and rub generously with salt; refrigerate for 1 hour. Rinse with cold water and place in a large soup pot. Add the parsnips, carrots, celery, dill, parsley sprigs, and water. Bring to a boil. Reduce the heat to medium-low and simmer for 1 hour, skimming occasionally to remove any scum that forms. Allow to cool, then cover and refrigerate overnight.

Skim the solidified fat from the surface with a skimmer or spoon. Warm the stock over medium heat. Remove the chicken and take the meat from the bones; tear into bite-size pieces. Strain the stock through a sieve lined with damp cheesecloth and discard the solids. Season with salt and ladle into serving bowls. Add some chicken, if desired, and top with minced parsley.

NOTE: A pullet is a chicken that is less than a year old.

RIBOLLITA

This hearty soup is made in the tradition of a Tuscan ribollita "reboiled" soup that always tastes better the next day and is finished with a healthy dose of olive oil stirred through at the end.

SERVES 6

5	ounces (140 g) dried cannellini beans
2	tablespoons (30 ml) plus ⅓ cup (80 ml) extra-virgin olive oil
2	medium onions, peeled and diced
8	garlic cloves, peeled and crushed
3	carrots, peeled and diced
3	celery ribs, diced
6	plum tomatoes, peeled and chopped
½	head cabbage, shredded
1	cup fresh flat-leaf parsley leaves
4	fresh thyme sprigs
8-10	cups (2–2.5 liters) low-sodium chicken broth
	Kosher salt and freshly ground black pepper
8	ounces (230 g) stale, rustic whole-wheat bread, roughly cut
1	bunch black kale (cavolo nero), thick stems removed

Per serving: 470 calories, 21 g total fat, 3 g saturated fat, 21 g protein, 56 g carbohydrates, 11 g dietary fiber, 340 mg sodium

Soak the beans in cold water for at least 8 hours or preferably overnight. Drain.

Heat 2 tablespoons (30 ml) of the oil in a large saucepan over low heat. Add the onions and garlic; cook for 3 minutes, or until fragrant. Add the beans, carrots, celery, tomatoes, cabbage, parsley, and thyme. Stir in 8 cups (2 liters) of the broth. Bring to a boil over medium heat. Reduce the heat and simmer for 1 hour, or until the beans are tender. Season to taste with salt and pepper.

Soak the bread in water until softened but not soggy and squeeze out the excess water. Add the bread and kale to the soup. Simmer for 20 minutes, stirring occasionally. Add more broth if needed, although the soup should be thick. Cool, cover, and refrigerate overnight.

To serve, reheat the soup, stirring to prevent it from sticking. Stir in the remaining ⅓ cup (80 ml) oil at the last minute.

CAVIAR AND POTATO TARTLETS

Depending on the size you make, these tartlets can be served as a first course or hors d'oeuvres with the Evelinda Cocktail (page 136). If making this as a large 9-inch (22 cm) pie, I place the potatoes on the bottom and then create circles of caviar around the top. Start with black caviar on the outside and then yellow and red; repeat until you get to the center and have a bull's-eye of red. Serve the pie cut into wedges.

I have no talent for making pie crust, so I buy pastry shells from a local bakery—which also saves time. These tartlets are delicious with any kind of caviar, from beluga to salmon.

SERVES 6

3/4 pound (340 g) small Yukon Gold potatoes

1 tablespoon salt

1 cup (230 g) fat-free sour cream

Baked pastry shells (see note)

About 3 ounces (90 g) beluga or osetra caviar or 5 ounces (145 g) salmon caviar (more if making a large pie)

Lemon wedges

Per serving: 250 calories, 9 g total fat, 2 g saturated fat, 9 g protein, 35 g carbohydrates, 0 g dietary fiber, 730 mg sodium

Put the potatoes in a medium saucepan and add enough cold water to cover them by 2 inches (5 cm). Bring to a boil over high heat. Add the salt, reduce the heat to medium, and boil the potatoes until they are tender, about 15 to 20 minutes. Drain the potatoes and let them cool slightly. Peel and cut into 1/4-inch (6 mm) slices. Transfer to a medium bowl and mix gently with 1/2 cup (115 g) of the sour cream.

Arrange the pastry shells on a large platter. Lay the potatoes in the pastry shells and top each tartlet with a layer of the remaining sour cream and a dollop of caviar. Serve at once with lemon wedges.

NOTE: Use eighteen 1 1/2-inch (4 cm) mini shells, six 3 1/2-inch (9 cm) tartlet shells, or one 9-inch (22 cm) pie crust. The last two require a fork and a knife.

SIMPLE VINAIGRETTE

The basic French dressing is very simple indeed: oil, wine vinegar or lemon juice, and pepper. Herbs and garlic are optional. Since there are so few ingredients, be sure to use the very best quality. You can make the dressing in your salad bowl, as below, or you can combine everything in a jar and shake it vigorously. Although the dressing will keep for a day or two, it is usually best when freshly made.

SERVES 6

1–2 tablespoons (15–30 ml) wine vinegar or a combination of vinegar and lemon juice

6–8 tablespoons (90–120 ml) extra-virgin olive oil, avocado oil, or other salad oil

Freshly ground black pepper

1 tablespoon minced shallot or scallion (optional)

¼ teaspoon dried herbs, such as tarragon or basil (optional)

Per serving: 120 calories, 14 g total fat, 2 g saturated fat, 0 g protein, 0 g carbohydrates, 0 g dietary fiber, 0 mg sodium

In a salad bowl, whisk together the vinegar and the lemon, if using. Then beat in the oil by droplets. Season with pepper. Stir in the shallots or scallions and the herbs, if using. Whisk in a little water if the dressing is too acidic.

OLIVE OIL

Olive oil is almost unique among oils in that it can be consumed in its crude form, without refinement. This has the effect of conserving all its vitamins, essential fatty acids, and other nutrients. Because it contains so many nutrients, including powerful antioxidants, real extra-virgin olive oil is beneficial to health and protects us from damage by free-radical oxidation.

Most people think that by purchasing "extra-virgin" olive oil they are automatically getting high-quality oil. To ensure the health benefits, find an extra-virgin oil that is cold pressed, unfiltered, and cloudy in appearance. It should be packaged in dark glass bottles to protect it from the damaging effects of light. When properly stored, real extra-virgin olive oil can last 2 to 3 years. However, it is best to purchase oil in small bottles and consume it within a year of purchase; this will also retain the best flavor. Store the oil away from both heat and light.

MY MUSTARD
VINAIGRETTE

All it takes is an empty jar, some great vegetable oil, and balsamic vinegar, and you can make this and keep it handy in the fridge. Eliminate the mustard and substitute ketchup to turn this dressing into a Russian dressing–style vinaigrette.

SERVES 6

1	tablespoon (15 ml) grainy Dijon mustard
2	shakes garlic powder
2	shakes onion powder
1	tablespoon (15 g) fat-free mayonnaise
2–3	teaspoons (10–15 ml) canola oil or garlic oil
1	tablespoon (15 ml) balsamic vinegar
¼	cup (60 ml) water
1	teaspoon superfine (caster) sugar

Place all ingredients in a jar and shake vigorously to combine. Keep in the refrigerator for up to a week.

Per serving: 25 calories, 1.5 g total fat, 0 g saturated fat, 1 g protein, 3 g carbohydrates, 0 g dietary fiber, 80 mg sodium

SALAD NIÇOISE

I add white anchovies, which are very interesting, to my
Niçoise salad, something that was suggested to me by my
friend Patricia Voyer, who runs a catering business in Palm
Beach called C'est Si Bon. The canned tuna that I think has the
best flavor is Progresso, and of course you can always use
fresh grilled tuna.

SERVES 4 TO 6

6	small red new potatoes
1	teaspoon caraway seeds
½	teaspoon kosher salt, plus extra for rubbing on beans
½	pound (230 g) haricots verts or other thin green beans
	Extra-virgin olive oil
4	large eggs
3	cans (12 ounces/340 g each) tuna packed in water
1	head romaine lettuce
1	green bell pepper, thinly sliced
3	tomatoes, cut into 6 wedges each
1	cup Niçoise or Greek olives
12	marinated white anchovies (optional)
	Simple Vinaigrette (page 148)

Per serving (based on 4 servings): 680 calories, 16 g
total fat, 3.5 g saturated fat, 75 g protein, 56 g carbohydrates, 9 g dietary fiber, 1,600 mg sodium

Place the potatoes and caraway seeds in a large
saucepan and add enough cold water to cover
by 1 inch (2.5 cm). Stir in the salt. Bring to a boil
and simmer for 5 minutes. Place the beans in a
steamer basket or colander. Set in the saucepan
with the potatoes. Cover and cook for 3 minutes,
or until the beans are crisp but tender.

Drain the beans and potatoes. Rinse the beans
with cold water and pat dry; rub with a little oil
and salt. Rub a sharp knife with oil to keep it from
sticking and slice the potatoes into halves or
quarters.

Put the eggs in a medium saucepan and add
water to cover by 1 inch (2.5 cm). Bring to a
simmer, cover, and cook for 9 minutes, until hard-
cooked. Drain and run under cool water for a
minute to make them easy to peel. Remove the
shells and halve the eggs. (You know you've
overcooked the eggs if there's a green ring on
the edge of the yolk.)

Drain the tuna and place in a small bowl, using a
fork to break into flaky pieces.

Separate the lettuce leaves and rinse well. Drain, dry, and tear the leaves. Arrange the lettuce, pepper, tomatoes, potatoes, beans, tuna, and eggs on a platter or divide among individual plates. Sprinkle with the olives and lay the anchovies decoratively on top, if using. Drizzle with the vinaigrette. Serve.

THE 6:30 P.M. DIET

The easiest way to drop pounds quickly is to dine early in the evening. If you do not eat anything afterward and drink only water before going to bed, you give your metabolism a 12-hour rest—enough time to burn off unwanted bulk.

As weight-loss diets go, this one is simple, effective, and healthy. I discovered it inadvertently, when my husband's bad back meant we could not accept dinner invitations and ate at home every evening for about 3 weeks. We were amazed to discover that, because we were cooking at home following low-fat recipes like ones in this book, we were both considerably trimmer afterward.

FAVA AND EDAMAME SALAD WITH TOASTED ALMONDS

Fava beans are in season in the early spring. Cooking and shelling fresh favas, which are also called broad beans, are a bit of work, but their flavor is distinctive, and I think it's worth the effort.

SERVES 4 TO 6

2   bunches watercress, trimmed

1   cup fresh mint leaves

2   cups shelled fresh fava beans, cooked and peeled

1   cup cooked shelled edamame

1   cup blanched almonds, toasted and coarsely chopped

¼   cup (60 ml) extra-virgin olive oil

   Juice of 2 lemons

   Kosher salt and freshly ground black pepper

¾   cup (170 g) low-fat ricotta cheese

In a large bowl, toss together the watercress, mint, fava beans, edamame, and almonds. Drizzle with the oil and lemon juice; season with salt and pepper. Toss to combine. Divide among individual salad bowls and sprinkle with the ricotta. Serve.

Per serving (based on 6 servings): 350 calories, 24 g total fat, 3.5 g saturated fat, 16 g protein, 23 g carbohydrates, 7 g dietary fiber, 140 mg sodium

ROOT VEGETABLE SALAD WITH TAHINI DRESSING

Tahini paste, which is made from sesame seeds, is a good source of essential fatty acids, copper, and calcium. Here, it lends a nutty taste to a wonderful mix of root vegetables. It is important to keep the tahini refrigerated to prevent it from turning rancid.

SERVES 4

DRESSING

¼	cup (60 ml) tahini
½	cup (120 ml) water
4	tablespoons (60 g) fat-free plain yogurt
	Juice of ½ lemon
2	garlic cloves, peeled and minced

SALAD

3	medium parsnips, peeled
3	medium carrots, peeled
3	medium beets, trimmed and peeled
1	medium celery root, peeled
3	red onions, peeled
8	small potatoes, halved
2	tablespoons (30 ml) extra-virgin olive oil
1	lemon, cut into quarters

Per serving: 550 calories, 17 g total fat, 2.5 g saturated fat, 15 g protein, 95 g carbohydrates, 14 g dietary fiber, 180 mg sodium

For the dressing: Place the tahini in a medium bowl. Gradually whisk in the water. Add the yogurt, lemon juice, and garlic. Stir to combine.

For the salad: Preheat the oven to 400°F (200°C).

Halve the parsnips and carrots crosswise, then cut in half lengthwise. (Cut any large pieces in half again lengthwise.) Place in a large roasting pan. Cut the beets, celery root, and onions into 1½-inch (4 cm) wedges; add to the pan. Add the potatoes.

Drizzle the vegetables with the oil and mix well. Roast for 1 hour, or until the vegetables are browned and tender when pierced. Divide among individual plates and drizzle with the dressing. Serve warm with the lemon wedges.

ASIAN PEAR, FENNEL, AND JÍCAMA SALAD

Serve this salad with some hearty walnut bread spread with Dijon mustard or a piece of cheese with a glass of sparkling grape juice. It would also be a great side salad to some smoked salmon.

SERVES 4 TO 6

3	Asian pears or firm ripe Bartletts
½	medium jícama, peeled
1	orange, juiced
2	fennel bulbs
6	ounces (170 g) fat-free plain yogurt
¾	cup shelled pistachio nuts, coarsely chopped (optional)

Per serving (based on 4 servings): 180 calories, 1 g total fat, 0 g saturated fat, 5 g protein, 44 g carbohydrates, 15 g dietary fiber, 90 mg sodium

Peel and core the pears. Cut the pears and jícama into thin julienne strips and sprinkle with half of the orange juice. Place in a large bowl.

Discard the thick outer layers from the fennel and slice the remainder into thin julienne strips. Add to the bowl. Stir in the yogurt and the remaining orange juice. Mix gently to coat. Scatter the pistachios on top, if using, to serve.

BALSAMIC ROAST BEETS

Beets, for all their health benefits, are not common at our table and are a good food to experiment with, as they can be eaten raw, steamed, roasted, or even juiced for an instant pick-me-up. This recipe adds balsamic vinegar, which enhances the natural sweetness of the beets.

SERVES 4 TO 6

4	large beets
1	teaspoon kosher salt, plus extra for seasoning
¼	cup (60 ml) balsamic vinegar
2	tablespoons (30 ml) extra-virgin olive oil
6	garlic cloves, peeled and crushed
	Freshly ground black pepper

Per serving (based on 4 servings): 120 calories, 7 g total fat, 1 g saturated fat, 2 g protein, 15 g carbohydrates, 2 g dietary fiber, 220 mg sodium

Place the beets and 1 teaspoon salt in a large saucepan; add cold water to cover. Bring to a boil, cover, and cook for 30 minutes, or until tender. Drain and run under cold water until cool enough to handle. Wearing plastic gloves to keep your hands clean, rub off the tough skin. Trim the beets and rinse.

Preheat the oven to 400°F (200°C). Cut each beet into pieces and place in a baking dish. Add the vinegar, oil, and garlic; stir to combine. Season with salt and pepper. Roast for 30 minutes and serve.

BALSAMIC VINEGAR

A true balsamic vinegar cannot be legally labeled *aceto balsamico tradizionale* until it has been aged 12 years.

The flavor should be smooth and full bodied, much the same as an aged brandy, rather than acidic. The taste should be the perfect balance of sweet and sour. The Italians feel that once balsamic vinegar has aged 50 years or more and has become thick, it should not be used in cooking but savored like an aged brandy or whiskey. Once the bottle is opened, it can be kept indefinitely if stored in a cool, dry place. Adding a dash of balsamic vinegar to mozzarella, tomatoes, and basil makes a very refined starter. Adding a dash to strawberries enhances their flavor greatly.

SWEET AND SOUR RED CABBAGE

Cabbage is a vegetable that is often only thought of for coleslaw, but it's actually very easy to cook. Sweet and sour cabbage is an Austrian dish that is usually served with Tafelspitz (boiled beef) or Wiener schnitzel, but it is also good paired with roast duck or chicken.

SERVES 4 TO 6

1	small head red cabbage
1	teaspoon (5 ml) canola oil
1	small onion, peeled, halved, and thinly sliced
¼	teaspoon caraway seeds
1	apple, shredded
⅓	cup raisins
1	cup (240 ml) water
¼	cup sugar
1	tablespoon citric acid (sour salt)

Per serving (based on 4 servings): 160 calories, 1.5 g total fat, 0 g saturated fat, 3 g protein, 39 g carbohydrates, 5 g dietary fiber, 45 mg sodium

Discard the outer leaves of the cabbage, cut into quarters, and remove the hard core. Finely shred the leaves. Warm the canola oil in a medium saucepan and sauté the onions for 2 to 3 minutes, until soft. Add the cabbage, caraway seeds, apple, raisins, and water to the saucepan with the onions. Bring to a boil. Stir in the sugar and citric acid. Cook for 12 minutes, until the cabbage is tender. Reduce the heat and allow to simmer until most of the water is evaporated. Place in a serving dish.

PUREED SWEET POTATOES

Sweet potatoes are a good source of the antioxidants beta-carotene and vitamin C. Though they're traditionally served to accompany the turkey at Thanksgiving, they're a lovely complement to any meat dish year-round.

SERVES 6

6	medium sweet potatoes
2	Rome apples, cored
½	teaspoon ground nutmeg
½	teaspoon ground cinnamon
1	tablespoon (15 ml) amaretto liqueur or 1 teaspoon (5 ml) almond extract

Per serving: 190 calories, 0 g total fat, 0 g saturated fat, 2 g protein, 43 g carbohydrates, 6 g dietary fiber, 45 mg sodium

SERVING TIP

Using a pastry bag gives an elegant presentation for any pureed vegetable. Fit the bag with a plain or fluted tip about ½ inch (1 cm) in diameter. Squeeze the puree into a circle and build into a cone shape for each serving.

Prick the sweet potatoes all over with a fork. Place on a paper towel and microwave on high power for 13 minutes; turn and microwave for an additional 13 minutes, until easily pierced with a fork. Set aside until cool enough to handle.

Place the apples in a microwave-safe dish, prick the skin, cover, and microwave on high power for 6 minutes, or until tender. Set aside until cool enough to handle.

Cut the sweet potatoes in half and use a spoon to scoop the flesh into a large bowl. Cut the apples in half and remove the skin. Mash using a fork or transfer to a food processor and process until smooth. Season with the nutmeg, cinnamon, and amaretto liqueur or almond extract. Transfer to an ovenproof dish and cover.

Preheat the oven to 250°F (120°C). Warm the puree in the oven for 10 minutes before serving.

NOTE: If using a conventional oven, preheat it to 400°F (200°C). Prick the sweet potatoes with a fork and place on a baking sheet. Bake for 30 minutes. Add the cored apples to the sheet and bake for 20 minutes, or until both the sweet potatoes and apples are soft.

STEAMED VEGETABLE MEDLEY WITH BREAD CRUMBS

Toasted bread crumbs always remind me of a meal my mother used to prepare, and they are delicious to sprinkle on any simple vegetable. A recipe for bread crumbs follows, or use good-quality store-bought.

SERVES 4

2	zucchini, cut into $\frac{1}{2}$-inch (1.3 cm) slices
1	cup small cauliflower florets
1	cup small broccoli florets
$\frac{1}{2}$	pound (230 g) green beans
1	tablespoon (15 ml) extra-virgin olive oil
4	tablespoons Basic Bread Crumbs (recipe follows)
	Kosher salt and freshly ground black pepper

Per serving (with bread crumbs): 80 calories, 4 g total fat, 0.5 g saturated fat, 4 g protein, 11 g carbohydrates, 4 g dietary fiber, 75 mg sodium

Place 1 inch (2.5 cm) of water in a saucepan and bring to a simmer over medium heat. Place the zucchini in a steamer basket and add to the pan. Cover and steam for 2 minutes. Carefully remove the lid and add the cauliflower and broccoli to the basket; steam for 4 minutes. Add the beans and steam for 2 minutes more, until the vegetables are tender.

Warm the oil in a medium skillet over low heat. Add the bread crumbs and cook, stirring constantly, for 2 minutes, or until lightly browned. Season with salt and pepper. Transfer to a small bowl.

Transfer the vegetables to a serving platter and sprinkle with the bread crumbs. Serve.

BASIC BREAD CRUMBS

MAKES 3 CUPS

6   slices whole-wheat, rye, or pumpernickel
     bread
     Olive oil cooking spray

Preheat the oven to 250°F (120°C).

Lightly coat both sides of each bread slice with the cooking spray. Place on a baking sheet and bake for 7 minutes, or until browned on top. Turn the slices over and bake until brown and very dry. Let cool.

Break the bread into pieces and place in a food processor. Process into fine crumbs. Store in an airtight container in the freezer and use as needed.

MOCK SNOWFLAKE "POTATOES"

This is another recipe that has everyone fooled, in that it tastes just like snowflake potatoes but is actually made from cauliflower. Cruciferous vegetables like cauliflower, along with broccoli, cabbage, and kale, are known for their sulforaphane, a compound that becomes active when these vegetables are chopped or chewed. These compounds may help the body protect itself against cancer.

SERVES 4 TO 6

1   cup (240 ml) Basic Vegetable Stock (page 139) or good-quality store-bought

1   medium onion, peeled and quartered

l   medium head cauliflower, cut into florets, including stems (about 4 cups)

4   tablespoons grated Parmesan cheese

1   teaspoon (5 g) butter, softened

Per serving (based on 4 servings): 80 calories, 2.5 g total fat, 1.5 g saturated fat, 5 g protein, 12 g carbohydrates, 4 g dietary fiber, 135 mg sodium

Bring the stock to a simmer in a medium saucepan. Add the onion and cauliflower and cook for 3 minutes, or until tender. Using a slotted spoon, remove the onion and cauliflower from the stock and drain on paper towels. (If desired, reserve the stock for another use.)

Place the cauliflower and onion in a food processor and blend until smooth. Add 2 tablespoons of the Parmesan and pulse to combine.

Preheat the broiler. Lightly butter an ovenproof dish and spoon in the cauliflower puree. Sprinkle the remaining 2 tablespoons Parmesan on top and broil for 3 minutes, until a golden brown crust is formed.

BRAISED FENNEL

Fennel contains its own unique combination of phytonutrients—including the flavonoids rutin, quercetin, and various kaempferol glycosides—that give it strong antioxidant activity. This recipe makes the fennel very tender and is delicious with any fish or light meat.

SERVES 4

2	tablespoons (30 ml) extra-virgin olive oil
2	large fennel bulbs, trimmed and cut into ¾-inch (2 cm) slices
½	onion, peeled and thinly sliced
2	large garlic cloves, peeled and sliced
1	cup (240 ml) water

Warm the oil in a large skillet over medium heat. Add the fennel, onion, and garlic; stir to mix. Add the water and cook for 6 to 8 minutes, until all the liquid has evaporated. Stir for several minutes, until the fennel is browned.

Per serving: 100 calories, 7 g total fat, 1 g saturated fat, 2 g protein, 10 g carbohydrates, 4 g dietary fiber, 65 mg sodium

CAULIFLOWER AND BROCCOLI GRATIN WITH GOAT CHEESE

The addition of goat cheese and yogurt adds high-quality protein and calcium to this healthy gratin.

SERVES 4

2	cups cauliflower florets
2	cups broccoli florets
4	ounces (115 g) soft goat cheese
½	cup (115 g) fat-free plain yogurt
¼	cup sliced almonds, toasted

Per serving: 150 calories, 9 g total fat, 4.5 g saturated fat, 10 g protein, 8 g carbohydrates, 3 g dietary fiber, 140 mg sodium

Preheat the broiler.

Place 1 inch (2.5 cm) of water in a saucepan and bring to a simmer over medium heat. Place the cauliflower and broccoli in a steamer basket and add to the pan. Cover and steam for 5 minutes, or until tender. Transfer to an ovenproof gratin dish.

In a small bowl, mix the goat cheese and yogurt to remove any lumps. Spoon over the vegetables. Broil for 3 to 5 minutes, or until the cheese begins to brown. Sprinkle with the almonds and serve.

BRUSSELS SPROUTS WITH ORANGE AND CHILI

These miniature green cabbages contain the same health-promoting nutrients as their larger cousins in the Brassica family: They are an excellent source of vitamin C, which supports immune function and promotes the manufacture of collagen. In addition, a cup of Brussels sprouts contains a healthy dose of beta-carotene, which plays an important role in defending the body against infection and promoting supple, glowing skin.

SERVES 4 TO 6

1	pound (450 g) Brussels sprouts
2	tablespoons (30 ml) extra-virgin olive oil
3	garlic cloves, peeled and minced
2	shallots, peeled and minced
¼	teaspoon crushed red pepper flakes (optional)
⅓	cup (80 ml) orange juice
	Kosher salt and freshly ground black pepper

Per serving (based on 4 servings): 130 calories, 7 g total fat, 1 g saturated fat, 4 g protein, 14 g carbohydrates, 4 g dietary fiber, 90 mg sodium

Trim the Brussels sprouts and use a paring knife to cut an X into the bottom of each.

Place 1 inch (2.5 cm) of water in a medium saucepan and bring to a simmer over medium heat. Place the sprouts in a steamer basket and add to the pan. Cover and cook for 5 to 7 minutes, or until tender.

Warm the oil in a large skillet over medium heat. Add the garlic, shallots, and pepper flakes, if using. Cook, stirring, for 2 minutes, or until fragrant. Add the sprouts and orange juice; cook, stirring occasionally, for 7 to 10 minutes, or until the liquid is absorbed and the sprouts have begun to caramelize in places. Season with salt and pepper and serve warm.

ROASTED BUCKWHEAT WITH CINNAMON

Buckwheat has a robust, nutlike flavor, perhaps the most distinctive of any food eaten as a grain. The particularly assertive taste of roasted buckwheat marries well with other hearty-flavored, densely textured foods, such as beef, root vegetables, cabbage, winter squash, roasted peppers, or eggplant. Nutritionally, the protein in buckwheat is of high quality because it contains all eight essential amino acids in good proportions.

SERVES 4 TO 6

2	tablespoons (30 ml) extra-virgin olive oil
1	large onion, peeled and finely chopped
2	garlic cloves, peeled and minced
½	teaspoon ground allspice
4	cups (1 liter) vegetable broth
2	bay leaves
1	cinnamon stick
2	cups roasted buckwheat (kasha)
	Kosher salt and freshly ground black pepper

Heat the oil in a medium saucepan over medium heat. Add the onion and garlic; cook, stirring, for 2 minutes, or until they begin to brown. Stir in the allspice. Add the broth, bay leaves, and cinnamon stick. Bring to a boil. Add the buckwheat, cover, and reduce the heat to low. Cook, without removing the lid, for 15 minutes, or until tender.

Remove and discard the bay leaves and cinnamon stick. Season with salt and pepper and spoon into a serving bowl.

Per serving (based on 4 servings): 400 calories, 9 g total fat, 1.5 g saturated fat, 11 g protein, 74 g carbohydrates, 10 g dietary fiber, 690 mg sodium

EGGPLANT CURRY

Supplying few calories and virtually no fat, its "meaty" texture makes eggplant a perfect vegetarian main-dish choice. This curry inspired by Eastern flavors would complement the Brown Rice with Orange (page 105).

SERVES 4 TO 6

1	green bell pepper
1	red bell pepper
3	tablespoons (45 ml) extra-virgin olive oil
⅛	teaspoon chili powder
4	cardamom pods, crushed
2	red onions, peeled and finely chopped
3	garlic cloves, peeled and minced
8	baby eggplant, halved lengthwise
3	large ripe tomatoes, peeled and chopped
¾	cup (180 ml) water
2	tablespoons (30 ml) lime juice
2	teaspoons ground coriander
2	teaspoons palm sugar or granulated sugar
	Kosher salt
1	teaspoon garam masala
	Chopped fresh cilantro leaves

Cut the peppers lengthwise into wide strips and then across into bite-size pieces.

Heat the oil in a large saucepan or wok over low heat. Add the chili powder and stir for a few seconds. Add the cardamom and onions; stir until golden. Add the peppers and garlic; cook, stirring, for about 3 minutes.

Add the eggplant and cook, stirring, for a few minutes more. Add the tomatoes, water, lime juice, coriander, and sugar. Season with salt. Cover and cook over low heat, stirring occasionally, until the eggplant is tender. Stir in the garam masala, and serve topped with the cilantro leaves.

Per serving (based on 4 servings): 230 calories, 11 g total fat, 1.5 g saturated fat, 5 g protein, 32 g carbohydrates, 10 g dietary fiber, 70 mg sodium

HERBED PUY LENTILS

Originating from Puy in France, these delicate peppery-flavored lentils retain their shape after cooking, which makes them perfect for this side. This dish pairs well with the Tuna with Fennel, Pistachio, and Lemon Spread (page 112).

SERVES 4

2	cups Puy lentils or French-style green lentils
1	tablespoon (15 ml) extra-virgin olive oil
3	garlic cloves, peeled and finely chopped
2	shallots, peeled and finely chopped
2	fresh thyme sprigs
3	cups (720 ml) vegetable broth
2	cups fresh flat-leaf parsley leaves
¼	cup (60 g) fat-free plain yogurt
1	lemon, cut into wedges

Rinse the lentils and pick over to remove any debris.

Heat the oil in a medium saucepan over medium heat. Add the garlic, shallots, and thyme. Cook, stirring, for 2 minutes, or until fragrant. Add the broth and bring to a boil. Stir in the lentils. Boil for 2 or 3 minutes and then reduce the heat to a simmer. Cover and cook for 20 minutes, or until tender.

Stir in the parsley and transfer to a serving bowl. Serve with the yogurt and lemon wedges on the side.

Per serving: 380 calories, 4 g total fat, 0.5 g saturated fat, 25 g protein, 65 g carbohydrates, 16 g dietary fiber, 570 mg sodium

LINGUINE WITH BROCCOLI SAUCE

This healthy sauce is made with broccoli, which like other cruciferous vegetables, contains phytochemicals with possible significant anti-cancer effects. It also boasts high levels of vitamin C and calcium.

SERVES 4

½ teaspoon kosher salt, plus extra for seasoning

1 large head broccoli, cut into florets (about 5 cups)

1 pound (450 g) fresh linguine, such as whole wheat or spinach

½ cup pine nuts

Grated zest and juice of 1 lemon

5 garlic cloves, peeled

⅓ cup (80 ml) chicken broth

⅓ cup (80 ml) plus 1 tablespoon (15 ml) extra-virgin olive oil

1 small onion, peeled and finely chopped

Freshly ground black pepper

4 tablespoons grated Parmesan cheese

½ cup fresh flat-leaf parsley leaves, chopped

Per serving: 700 calories, 38 g total fat, 6 g saturated fat, 21 g protein, 75 g carbohydrates, 7 g dietary fiber, 380 mg sodium

Bring a large saucepan of water to a boil. Add 1 teaspoon salt and the broccoli. Cook for 1 minute. Remove the broccoli with a slotted spoon and transfer to a bowl of ice water. Drain and set aside.

Cook the linguine in the boiling water for 4 to 5 minutes, until al dente. Drain and set aside.

Place the broccoli in a food processor or blender. Add the pine nuts, lemon zest and juice, 3 garlic cloves, chicken broth, and ⅓ cup (80 ml) of the oil. Puree.

Mince the remaining 2 garlic cloves. Heat the remaining 1 tablespoon (15 ml) oil in a large skillet. Add the onion and garlic; cook, stirring, for 1 minute, or until translucent. Add the broccoli sauce and cook, stirring, for 2 minutes. Season with salt and pepper.

Add the linguine and toss to coat. Divide among individual bowls. Top each serving with Parmesan and parsley.

MY TOMATO SAUCE

My fail-safe recipe, which uses no oil, doesn't miss a beat for flavor and is a great way to get children to eat vegetables.

SERVES 4

1	medium onion, peeled and finely chopped
2	celery ribs, finely chopped
1	small green bell pepper, finely chopped
2	garlic cloves, peeled and finely chopped
1	can (28 ounces/800 g) Italian-style peeled tomatoes
6	small mushrooms, sliced
1	medium carrot, peeled and finely grated
2	tablespoons chopped fresh basil
1	teaspoon chopped fresh oregano
1	tablespoon sugar (optional)

Per serving: 90 calories, 0 g total fat, 0 g saturated fat, 3 g protein, 19 g carbohydrates, 5 g dietary fiber, 460 mg sodium

Place 1 inch (2.5 cm) of water in a large nonstick saucepan. Add the onion, celery, pepper, and garlic. Bring to a simmer over medium heat and cook for 7 minutes, or until the vegetables are tender and the water has evaporated. Add the tomatoes and their juice, mushrooms, carrot, basil, and oregano; simmer over low heat for at least 25 minutes, until the sauce becomes rich in color. Add the sugar, if desired, to reduce the acidity.

TOMATO SAUCE

To cut down on the acidity in tomato sauce or soup, you can add a little sugar. This is something Estée always did, and much to the dismay of many waiters I do it too! The benefits to the flavor far outweigh the 16 calories in a teaspoon of sugar.

WILD RICE WITH DRIED CHERRIES AND NUTS

Wild rice really isn't rice at all, but a long-grain marsh grass native to the Great Lakes region of North America. Wild rice has twice the protein and fiber of brown rice but less calcium and iron. When it is cooked and used like rice, it has a nutty flavor and chewy texture and is a good source of whole grain.

SERVES 6

2	cups wild rice
2	tablespoons (30 ml) extra-virgin olive oil
1	medium onion, peeled and finely chopped
2	garlic cloves, peeled and minced
½	cup dried cherries, chopped
3	cups (720 ml) vegetable or low-sodium chicken broth
1	cup (240 ml) water
½	cup sliced almonds or pine nuts
	Kosher salt and freshly ground black pepper

Per serving: 350 calories, 10 g total fat, 1.5 g saturated fat, 13 g protein, 54 g carbohydrates, 6 g dietary fiber, 80 mg sodium

Place the rice in a large sieve and rinse with cold water; drain. Heat the oil in a large saucepan over medium heat. Add the onion and garlic; cook, stirring occasionally, for 5 minutes, until golden. Add the cherries and rice; cook, stirring, for 3 minutes, or until fragrant.

Stir in the broth and water; bring to a boil. Reduce the heat to low, cover, and simmer for 1 to 1¼ hours, or until the rice is tender and the grains split open.

Place the almonds or pine nuts in a medium skillet and stir over medium heat for 2 minutes, or until golden. Gently stir into the rice and season with the salt and pepper. Transfer to a bowl to serve.

PEARL BARLEY AND PORCINI RISOTTO

Using barley in this recipe is a nice change from a traditional risotto, which is made from arborio rice. The nutty flavor of the barley absorbs the flavor of the mushrooms to make a more chewy but flavorful risotto that is high in fiber and a good source of whole grains.

SERVES 4 TO 6

1½	ounces (45 g) dried porcini mushrooms (about 12)
1	cup (240 ml) boiling water
5	cups (1.2 liters) Basic Vegetable Stock (page 139) or low-sodium chicken broth
1	cup (240 ml) red wine
1	star anise
1	tablespoon (15 ml) extra-virgin olive oil
1	shallot, peeled and finely chopped
2	garlic cloves, peeled and finely chopped
¼	cup dried currants
1	fresh rosemary sprig
1½	cups pearl barley
	Kosher salt and freshly ground black pepper

Per serving (based on 4 servings): 470 calories, 6 g total fat, 1.5 g saturated fat, 18 g protein, 73 g carbohydrates, 15 g dietary fiber, 260 mg sodium

Place the porcini in a small bowl and cover with the boiling water. Set aside to soak.

In a medium saucepan, combine the stock, wine, and star anise. Bring to a boil over high heat, then reduce the heat to low.

Heat the oil in a large saucepan over medium heat. Add the shallot, garlic, currants, and rosemary; cook until the shallot is lightly browned. Add the barley and cook for 1 minute. Ladle in enough stock to just cover the barley; simmer, stirring, until most of the liquid is absorbed Repeat the process until all the liquid is used, about 35 to 40 minutes.

Stir in the porcini and soaking liquid. Simmer, stirring, until the liquid is absorbed, about 3 to 4 minutes. Remove and discard the rosemary and star anise. Season with salt and pepper. Serve.

SALMON MOUSSE

This mousse is one of my son Gary's favorites. I serve it as an hors d'oeurve with assorted crudités such as celery, jícama, cherry tomatoes, and blanched snow peas. As a first course, slice the mousse onto a bed of arugula or radicchio, with some tartar sauce and a wedge of lemon on the side.

Salmon is one of the best fish sources for the nutritionally valuable omega-3 fatty acids. The numerous health benefits range from reducing the risk of heart disease and cancer to improving the health and tone of the skin.

SERVES 8 AS AN HORS D'OEUVRE

2½	cups (600 ml) water
4	fresh dill sprigs
1	pound (450 g) skinless wild salmon fillets or 1 can (14¾ ounces/425 g) sockeye salmon, drained
1	envelope unflavored gelatin
¼	cup (60 g) tomato paste
⅔	cup (145 g) fat-free sour cream
½	cup (115 g) fat-free plain yogurt (see note)
2	tablespoons grated onion
2	teaspoons grated lemon zest
3	tablespoons (45 ml) lemon juice
	Kosher salt and freshly ground black pepper

Per serving: 120 calories, 3.5 g total fat, 0.5 g saturated fat, 15 g protein, 7 g carbohydrates, 0 g dietary fiber, 90 mg sodium

Place 2 cups (480 ml) of the water and the dill in a large nonstick skillet. Bring to a boil over medium heat. Add the fresh salmon. Reduce the heat to low, cover, and cook for 12 minutes, or until just cooked through, turning the salmon over after 6 minutes. Lift from the cooking liquid and cool to room temperature.

Place the remaining ½ cup (120 ml) water in a heatproof measuring cup and sprinkle with the gelatin. Let stand for 5 minutes, or until softened. Set the cup in a small saucepan of simmering water and heat until the gelatin melts.

Place the cooked or canned salmon, tomato paste, sour cream, yogurt, onion, lemon zest, lemon juice, and gelatin in a food processor and pulse until the mixture is smooth. Season with salt and pepper.

Pour the salmon mixture into a ring mold or soufflé dish. Cover and chill for at least 8 hours or overnight. To unmold, dip the mold into a large pan of hot water for 5 seconds and run a thin knife around the edge. Invert a platter over the mold and invert the mousse onto the platter. Garnish the platter as desired and serve.

NOTE: The fat-free sour cream and the fat-free yogurt can be replaced with 1¼ cups (285 g) of fat-free mayonnaise.

ELIZABETH HURLEY'S SALMON TARTARE

Elizabeth Hurley is not only a spokesmodel for Estée Lauder but also the model spokesperson for The Breast Cancer Research Foundation and a true friend. This is her recipe in her words: "We often serve Indian food at my dinner parties, and so I'm always looking for light starters. This tartare is perfect and absolutely delicious. You can decide what quantity to make, but I plan on about 2 heaped tablespoons per person."

SERVES 4

4	ounces (115 g) smoked salmon, cut into very fine dice
4	ounces (115 g) sashimi-quality salmon, cut into very fine dice
	Juice of 1 lemon
2	teaspoons (10 g) mayonnaise (mix in a touch of wasabi if you like)
1	tablespoon chopped fresh chives
	Kosher salt and freshly ground black pepper
	Balsamic vinegar
	Watercress or fresh flat-leaf parsley sprigs
	Lemon wedges

In a medium bowl, mix the salmon, lemon juice, mayonnaise, and chives. Season with salt and pepper. Taste and add more of something if you think it needs it.

Find a small, round cookie cutter and pack the salmon tartare tightly into the cutter in the middle of each plate. Remove the cutter and the tartare should stand alone and look very professional!

Drip balsamic vinegar onto the plates. Serve garnished with the watercress or parsley and lemon wedges.

Per serving: 120 calories, 6 g total fat, 1 g saturated fat, 12 g protein, 4 g carbohydrates, 0 g dietary fiber, 30 mg sodium

SALMON SAINT NELIDA

This recipe was originally created by Nelly, who works for me and cooks like a saint. It was once served to 900 people at The Breast Cancer Research Foundation dinner at the Waldorf-Astoria Hotel.

SERVES 6

6   garlic cloves, peeled and minced

½   medium onion, peeled and minced

2   tablespoons peeled and minced fresh ginger

½   lemon, juiced

1   tablespoon (15 ml) toasted sesame oil

2   tablespoons (30 ml) rice wine vinegar

½   cup (120 ml) thick teriyaki sauce

1   teaspoon brown sugar

6   salmon fillets, 6 ounces (170 g) each

Per serving: 370 calories, 21 g total fat, 4 g saturated fat, 36 g protein, 8 g carbohydrates, 0 g dietary fiber, 1,020 mg sodium

Put the garlic, onion, and ginger in a bowl and stir in the lemon juice, sesame oil, rice wine vinegar, teriyaki sauce, and sugar to combine.

Lay the salmon fillets, skin side down, in a single layer in a shallow glass dish. Pour the glaze over the fillets. Cover and refrigerate for 30 minutes.

Preheat the broiler. Place the salmon in a broiler-safe pan and spoon the glaze over the fillets so each has some ginger, garlic, and onion on top to create a crust. Broil 3 to 4 inches (7.5 to 10 cm) from the heat for 10 to 12 minutes, or until the fish is opaque and has a brown crust.

RED SNAPPER WITH FENNEL

Fennel seeds enhance the flavor of the fish and in India are often chewed after a meal to aid digestion. They give the fish a most unusual taste that most people admire very much. Serve this with braised fennel, pureed carrots, or some sugar snap peas.

SERVES 4

2	teaspoons fennel seeds
4	snapper fillets, 6 ounces (170 g) each
	Kosher salt and freshly ground black pepper
	Juice of 1 large lemon
1	tablespoon (15 ml) extra-virgin olive oil
1	lemon, thinly sliced or cut into wedges

Per serving: 210 calories, 6 g total fat, 1 g saturated fat, 35 g protein, 0 g carbohydrates, 3 g dietary fiber, 170 mg sodium

Place the fennel seeds in a small skillet and toast over medium heat for 1 to 2 minutes, or until fragrant. Roughly crush the seeds using a mortar and pestle or a rolling pin.

Preheat the broiler to medium-high. Place the fish in a single layer in an ovenproof baking dish and sprinkle with the fennel. Season with salt and pepper and then drizzle with the lemon juice and oil.

Broil the fish until opaque in the center, about 5 minutes; do not turn the pieces. Transfer the fish to serving plates. Serve immediately with the lemon slices or wedges.

HALIBUT WITH PARSLEY SAUCE

Refreshing and healthy, this easy dish calls for simple side dishes like Herbed Puy Lentils (page 168) and Steamed Asparagus with Basic Aioli (page 122). Cold-water fish like halibut are a rich source of the omega-3 essential fats and are a good alternative to salmon as a source of these vital nutrients.

SERVES 6

6	halibut fillets, 6 ounces (170 g) each
6	tablespoons (90 ml) extra-virgin olive oil
	Freshly ground black pepper
3	garlic cloves, peeled
1/2	teaspoon salt, plus extra for seasoning
2	tablespoons (30 ml) hot water
	Juice of 2 lemons
1/4	cup finely chopped fresh flat-leaf parsley
2	tablespoons finely chopped fresh oregano

Per serving: 320 calories, 18 g total fat, 2.5 g saturated fat, 36 g protein, 2 g carbohydrates, 0 g dietary fiber, 135 mg sodium

Place the fish in a single layer in a shallow dish. Coat all over with 3 tablespoons (45 ml) of the oil and season lightly with salt and pepper.

In a small bowl, crush together the garlic and 1/2 teaspoon salt to form a smooth paste. Whisk in the water, lemon juice, and the remaining 3 tablespoons (45 ml) oil to form an emulsified sauce. Stir in the parsley and oregano.

Heat a large nonstick skillet over medium heat. Add the fish and cook for 5 minutes, turning once. Transfer to plates and spoon some sauce over each serving.

EASY BAKED FISH

In the area of food and phytonutrient research, the studies on the lycopene in tomatoes have been extensive. This carotenoid has been shown to have antioxidant and cancer-preventing properties. The tomatoes become sweet when baked, so it's a good way to get children to eat fish.

SERVES 6

6	cod, sole, or flounder fillets, 6 ounces (170 g) each
	Juice of 1 lemon
2	tablespoons (30 ml) extra-virgin olive oil
2	medium red onions, peeled and sliced
2	garlic cloves, peeled and finely chopped
1	cup chopped fresh flat-leaf parsley
6	large tomatoes, chopped
½	cup (120 ml) water
3	tablespoons fresh lemon thyme leaves
3	medium tomatoes, thinly sliced
1	lemon, thinly sliced

Per serving: 260 calories, 7 g total fat, 1 g saturated fat, 33 g protein, 18 g carbohydrates, 4 g dietary fiber, 120 mg sodium

Preheat the oven to 350°F (180°C).

Place the fillets in a lightly oiled baking dish and drizzle with the lemon juice.

Warm 1 tablespoon (15 ml) of the oil in a large skillet over medium heat. Add the onions and garlic and cook for 3 minutes, or until translucent. Add the parsley, chopped tomatoes, and water. Simmer for 10 minutes, stirring occasionally.

Pour the tomato mixture over the fish, sprinkle with the thyme, and top each fillet with overlapping tomato and lemon slices. Drizzle with the remaining 1 tablespoon (15 ml) oil. Cover and bake for 15 minutes, or until the fish is opaque in the center when tested with a knife. Serve warm.

SEA BASS WITH GREEN AIOLI

Olive oil is the main ingredient of aioli, which is similar to a garlic mayonnaise. Extra-virgin olive oil, from the first pressing of the olives, contains higher levels of antioxidants, particularly vitamin E and phenols, because it is less processed then regular olive oil. A simple baked potato makes a nice accompaniment to the sea bass.

SERVES 6

1	large egg
1/3	cup lightly packed fresh mint, basil, or flat-leaf parsley leaves
1	teaspoon grated lemon zest
2–4	garlic cloves, peeled
1/8	teaspoon kosher salt, plus extra for seasoning
1/2	cup (120 ml) extra-virgin olive oil, plus extra for the fish
6	sea bass fillets with skin, 6 ounces (170 g) each
	Freshly ground black pepper
1	lime, cut into wedges

Per serving: 350 calories, 23 g total fat, 3.5 g saturated fat, 33 g protein, 1 g carbohydrates, 0 g dietary fiber, 190 mg sodium

Combine the egg; mint, basil, or parsley; lemon zest and juice, garlic; and 1/8 teaspoon salt in a blender or food processor. Process until well blended.

With the machine running, gradually add 1 cup (240 ml) of the oil in a thin, steady stream until all is incorporated. Set the aioli aside.

Preheat the broiler. Place the fish, skin side down, on a rimmed baking sheet and brush with oil. Season with salt and pepper. Broil 7 inches (18 cm) from the heat, without turning, for 5 to 6 minutes, or until crisp on the top and opaque in the center when tested with a knife.

Serve with the green aioli and lime wedges.

SAUTÉED BAY SCALLOPS

If you are looking for fast and easy, this scallop recipe is for you! Bay scallops are small and very sweet. They are in season from November to March. I serve the scallops with long-grain white or brown rice and wedges of lemon.

SERVES 4

1½	pounds (680 g) bay scallops
	Ground paprika
1	tablespoon (15 ml) light olive oil
1	teaspoon (5 g) butter (see note)
1	tablespoon peeled and minced shallot
1	garlic clove, peeled and minced
¼	cup (60 ml) white wine
1	tablespoon (15 ml) lemon juice

Per serving: 200 calories, 6 g total fat, 1 g saturated fat, 29 g protein, 5 g carbohydrates, 0 g dietary fiber, 280 mg sodium

Rinse the scallops with cold water and pat dry. Sprinkle lightly with the paprika.

Heat the oil and butter in a large nonstick skillet over medium-high heat for about 1 minute. Add the scallops to the skillet, a few at a time to avoid crowding, and cook for 1 minute per side, or until golden brown on the outside but still translucent in the middle. Transfer the scallops to a heated platter and cover to keep warm.

Add the shallot and garlic to the skillet and cook for 1 minute. Add the wine and lemon juice and cook for another 2 minutes. Return the scallops to the skillet and toss with the sauce. Serve immediately.

NOTE: You can omit the butter and sauté the scallops in oil alone, but the butter gives them a nice golden brown color.

SCALLOPS EN PAPILLOTE

En papillote means the scallops are wrapped in parchment paper to cook. It is a very healthy way to cook seafood as it retains the moisture and flavor and makes for an interesting presentation.

SERVES 4

2	cups (480 ml) water
½	teaspoon kosher salt, plus extra for seasoning
½	cup spelt grain
2	cups sliced shiitake mushroom caps
1	tablespoon (15 ml) extra-virgin olive oil
	Grated zest and juice of ½ orange
1	tablespoon fresh thyme leaves
	Freshly ground black pepper
1½	pounds (680 g) sea scallops, rinsed and patted dry

Per serving: 270 calories, 2 g total fat, 0 g saturated fat, 32 g protein, 33 g carbohydrates, 2 g dietary fiber, 540 mg sodium

Bring the water and ½ teaspoon salt to a boil in a medium saucepan. Add the spelt and simmer for 45 minutes, until tender but not mushy. Drain and place in a large bowl. Add the mushrooms, oil, orange juice, and thyme. Season with salt and pepper.

Preheat the oven to 400°F (200°C).

Tear four 15-inch (38 cm) squares of parchment paper and arrange two each on two baking sheets. Spoon equal portions of the spelt mixture into the center of each square. Divide the scallops equally on top of the spelt and sprinkle with the orange zest. Top with four more squares of parchment and fold the edges over several times to seal.

Bake for 15 minutes. Transfer each packet to a plate and serve with a sharp knife to slit the packets, being careful of the steam that will escape.

PASTA WITH CHICKEN AND SUN-DRIED TOMATOES

Years ago Leonard and I were in California and went to an Italian restaurant in Malibu. They served the most incredible chicken with sun-dried tomatoes, which at the time were new to me. This is my version of a meal we still enjoy today.

SERVES 4 TO 6

2½	ounces (175 g) dried porcini or portobello mushrooms
2	cups (480 ml) boiling water
3	fresh flat-leaf parsley sprigs
2	fresh thyme sprigs
1	piece (3 inches/7.5 cm) celery rib
3	cups (720 ml) cold water
1	cup (240 ml) chicken broth
8	ounces (230 g) cremini mushrooms, caps and stems chopped separately
1	large leek, cleaned and chopped (white and light green parts only)
6	black peppercorns, cracked
10	sun-dried tomatoes
1	pound (450 g) skinless, boneless chicken breasts or thighs
½	pound (230 g) whole-wheat spaghetti
	Kosher salt
	Balsamic vinegar

Per serving (based on 4 servings): 430 calories, 2.5 g total fat, 0.5 g saturated fat, 42 g protein, 61 g carbohydrates, 13 g dietary fiber, 350 mg sodium

Place the dried mushrooms in a bowl and add the boiling water. Let stand for 15 minutes, or until softened. Lift out the mushrooms and squeeze excess liquid back into the bowl. Rinse to remove any grit and chop finely. Place in a large saucepan.

Line a sieve with a damp paper towel and strain the soaking liquid into the saucepan.

Tuck the parsley and thyme sprigs into the celery cavity, tie together with string, and add to the saucepan. Add 2 cups (480 ml) of the cold water, the chicken broth, cremini stems, leek, and peppercorns. Bring to a simmer, stirring occasionally. Reduce the heat, partially cover, and cook at a bare simmer for 30 minutes.

Line the sieve with a double thickness of rinsed cheesecloth and strain the liquid into a large bowl. Press on the solids to remove all the broth; discard the solids.

Pour half of the broth into a large skillet. Add the tomatoes, chicken, and cremini caps. Cover and simmer for 10 minutes, or until the chicken is just cooked. Remove the chicken and tomatoes and slice finely. Return to the broth.

Bring the remaining broth and 1 cup (240 ml) cold water to a boil in a large saucepan. Add the spaghetti and cook for 10 minutes, or until al dente. Divide the spaghetti, broth, and chicken mixture among soup bowls. Season with salt and serve with a drizzle of vinegar, if desired.

CLEANING MUSHROOMS

Use as little water as possible with mushrooms, since they tend to absorb water. Remove any dirt by rubbing gently with a soft cloth or brush. If the mushrooms are very dirty, put them in a colander and rinse with cold water; make sure to drain them well on paper towels. Remove woody stems, like those of shiitake, or just trim the discolored stem ends of tender button mushrooms.

CHINESE FONDUE WITH FOUR SAUCES

An unusual dish that we had at the Kulm Hotel in St. Moritz in 1975 has become a favorite for entertaining, especially in winter after skiing. When I serve this dish, I usually start with a salad as the vegetable course.

SERVES 4 TO 6

Chive Sauce (recipe follows)

Curry Sauce (recipe follows)

Honey Mustard Sauce (recipe follows)

Chili Sauce (recipe follows)

4 cups (1 liter) low-sodium chicken broth

1½ pounds (680 g) boneless, skinless poultry or meat, such as chicken breast, veal, and filet mignon, sliced into paper-thin strips

8 ounces (230 g) spaghetti or soba noodles

Per serving (based on 4 servings with chicken and 4 sauces): 610 calories, 6 g total fat, 1 g saturated fat, 57 g protein, 84 g carbohydrates, 3 g dietary fiber, 1,406 mg sodium

Make the dipping sauces and set aside.

Pour the broth into a fondue pot. Most fondue pots serve 4 people. Place the fondue pot on the table with its heat source centered below the bottom of the pot. Bring the broth to a simmer.

Place the raw meat on several communal plates on the table. Have small bowls of the sauces for each person.

Using long fondue forks, spear the meat and dip into the simmering broth to cook for 1 to 2 minutes, until the meat is cooked through. Use the dinner fork to remove the meat from the hot fondue fork to the dinner plates. Dip in the sauce of choice. Place the next piece of meat on the fondue fork and cook while you enjoy the last piece and so on.

When all the meat has been cooked, take the fondue pot back to the kitchen and transfer the broth to a large pot. Bring to a boil, add the pasta, and cook until al dente. Serve the noodles with a little broth in soup bowls.

FOUR SAUCES

CHIVE SAUCE

1	cup (230 g) fat-free sour cream
4	tablespoons finely chopped fresh chives
2	tablespoons finely chopped scallion (white and green parts)
½	small red onion, peeled and finely chopped

Mix the ingredients in a small bowl.

CURRY SAUCE

1	cup (230 g) fat-free plain yogurt
¼	teaspoon curry powder
¼	teaspoon mustard powder

Mix the ingredients in a small bowl.

HONEY MUSTARD SAUCE

½	cup (120 ml) honey mustard
1	small lemon, juiced

Mix the ingredients in a small bowl.

CHILI SAUCE

3	tablespoons (45 ml) low-sodium soy sauce
4	tablespoons (60 ml) sweet chili sauce
2	garlic cloves, peeled and minced
2	limes, juiced

Mix the ingredients in a small bowl.

THE BEST ROAST CHICKEN

Something I learned from my visits to France about roasting chickens is to make sure you have plenty of time to roast the bird very slowly in the oven. It produces a most delicious result. And that way, there is time to enjoy conversation with the family while the meal cooks.

SERVES 4

1	roasting chicken, about 4–5 pounds (2–2.3 kg)
$\frac{1}{2}$	teaspoon kosher salt
$\frac{1}{4}$	teaspoon freshly ground black pepper

Per serving (without skin): 480 calories, 18 g total fat, 5 g saturated fat, 74 g protein, 0 g carbohydrates, 0 g dietary fiber, 320 mg sodium

ROAST CHICKEN

The best way to tell if a chicken is cooked properly is to use a meat thermometer. The internal temperature of a whole chicken should reach 180°F (80°C). Another check for doneness is to pierce or make a slit in the thickest part of the meat to see if the juices run clear. If they're clear and not pink, your chicken is done. I find also that if the thigh bone moves back and forth easily when wiggled, the chicken is usually ready.

Preheat the oven to 275°F (135°C). Remove the giblets from the chicken's cavity (save for stock, if you like—but don't include the liver, which would make the stock bitter). Pull any loose fat from around the opening. Rinse the bird inside and out with cold water and pat dry. Sprinkle inside and out with the salt and pepper.

Place the chicken, breast side down, on a V-shaped roasting rack (or a flat rack) and set the rack in a roasting pan just larger than the rack. Roast for $1\frac{1}{2}$ hours. Turn the bird breast side up. Continue roasting for 1 hour and 40 minutes for a 4-pound chicken. For larger birds, add another 10 minutes for each additional pound.

The chicken is done when the leg wiggles freely in its joint and when the juices run clear from the thigh when you prick it. An instant-read thermometer inserted into the lower meaty part of the thigh should register 170°F (75°C). Set the chicken on a warm platter to rest for 10 minutes before carving. Serving the meat with the skin on makes for a nice presentation, but I don't recommend eating the skin as it is high in fat and calories.

EASY "ALL IN ONE" STEWED CHICKEN

This recipe calls for a cut-up whole chicken, but you can certainly use legs, thighs, or breast meat. Leave a 2-inch (5 cm) piece of breast meat attached to each wing. This makes the wing section a more generous portion.

SERVES 4

1	chicken, about 3 pounds (1.4 kg), cut into 8 pieces
	Kosher salt and freshly ground black pepper
1	onion, peeled and finely chopped
3	large carrots, peeled and finely chopped
3	celery ribs, finely chopped
½	green bell pepper, finely chopped
1	cup (240 ml) water
1	cup fresh or frozen peas
8	cremini mushrooms, sliced

Per serving (without skin): 300 calories, 6 g total fat, 1.5 g saturated fat, 43 g protein, 16 g carbohydrates, 5 g dietary fiber, 250 mg sodium

Rinse the chicken with cold water and pat dry. Season with salt and black pepper.

Heat a large nonstick skillet over medium-high heat. Add the chicken, skin side down, and brown, turning the pieces with tongs. Transfer to a platter lined with paper towels. Discard any remaining fat from the skillet, leaving a thin layer in which to cook the vegetables.

Return the chicken to the skillet, skin side up, and move it to the back of the pan away from direct heat. Add the onion, carrots, celery, and bell pepper to the skillet and cook over medium-high heat for 5 minutes, or until the onions begin to brown. Add the water, reduce the heat to low, partially cover, and simmer for 20 to 30 minutes, or until the chicken is cooked through.

Cook uncovered for 10 minutes to concentrate the sauce. Add the peas and mushrooms for the last 3 minutes of cooking time. Spoon off any fat that may rise to the surface. When serving, you may want to leave the skin on for presentation, but I don't recommend eating the skin as it is high in fat and calories.

SIGNATURE ROAST DUCK

Served with wild rice and peas, this duck is requested by many of our friends. This recipe was given to me when I first married Leonard by a lovely lady named Ida, who worked with Estée and Joe in their home. She told me it was given to her by an elderly lady when she was very young. It is important to remember that you need one duck for every two people, which I did not realize back then. It caused me great embarrassment once when as a newlywed I asked another couple to dinner to share a single duck. I was inexperienced in the kitchen!

SERVES 4

2	ducks, about 5½ pounds (2.5 kg) each
2	teaspoons kosher salt
½	teaspoon freshly ground black pepper
2	tablespoons (30 ml) lemon juice
1	teaspoon (5 ml) extra-virgin olive oil
1	Bermuda or Spanish onion, peeled and cut into 1-inch (2.5 cm) pieces
1	jar (8 ounces/230 g) Major Grey chutney

Per serving (without skin): 560 calories, 23 g total fat, 8 g saturated fat, 47 g protein, 36 g carbohydrates, 0 g dietary fiber, 1,490 mg sodium

Preheat the oven to 375°F (190°C).

Remove any prickly feather stubs with a strawberry huller or tweezers and rinse each duck thoroughly, inside and out, with cold water. Pat dry with paper towels. Season the ducks inside and out with salt and pepper, massaging each duck with 1 tablespoon (15 ml) of the lemon juice to dissolve the salt and spread it evenly over the skin. Truss the birds and tuck the wing tips under. Place breast side up on a nonstick roasting rack fitted in a large roasting pan.

Roast the ducks for 2 to 2½ hours; every 30 minutes or so, prick the outside skin all over with a two-pronged carving fork with the prongs pointing up (this will prick only the fat just under the skin to keep the meat moist) and rotate the pan. It may seem like a bother, but it's the best way to ensure an even crispy skin. Remove accumulated fat occasionally with a bulb baster. The legs will wiggle easily when the bird is done and an instant-read thermometer will register about 180°F (80°C) when inserted into the thigh. The skin should be crisp and golden brown.

Remove the ducks from the oven, discard trussing strings, and place on a serving platter. Let sit for 10 minutes before carving.

While duck is roasting in the oven, heat the oil in a large nonstick skillet over medium heat. Add the onion and cook, adding a little water so it does not brown, until translucent, about 3 minutes. Add the chutney and stir to combine. Continue to cook, stirring, for 30 minutes, or until the sauce thickens and becomes very dark.

Carve the ducks and serve with the sauce on the side. Although you may want to leave the skin on for a nice presentation, I don't recommend eating the skin as it is high in fat and calories.

CRANBERRY RELISH

My family adores this relish, which contains the peel of the oranges. It's not only our favorite with roasted turkey but is very good with duck, capon, or chicken. The relish can be made several days in advance.

SERVES 6

1	pound (450 g) fresh cranberries
2	medium navel oranges, washed and cut into large pieces
½	cup sugar (more if needed)
¼	teaspoon ground cinnamon
	Pinch of ground nutmeg

Put half of the cranberries and half of the oranges into a food processor and process until very finely chopped. Transfer to a bowl. Repeat with the remaining cranberries and oranges. Taste the mixture and stir in the sugar, adjusting the amount to your palate. Mix in the cinnamon and nutmeg. Cover and refrigerate until needed.

Per serving: 120 calories, 0 g total fat, 0 g saturated fat, 1 g protein, 32 g carbohydrates, 5 g dietary fiber, 0 mg sodium

SESAME MAYONNAISE

Many people are probably familiar with sesame oil because it gives some Asian foods their characteristic flavor. It will give a distinctive nutty flavor to salad dressings and stir-fries. Sesame oil is rich in vitamin E, an antioxidant known to help lower cholesterol. Sesame oil also contains magnesium, copper, calcium, iron, and vitamin B_6.

MAKES 1 CUP (240 ML)

1	cup (240 ml) extra-virgin olive oil
2	teaspoons (10 ml) toasted sesame oil
2	large egg yolks
$\frac{1}{2}$	teaspoon salt
2	tablespoons (30 ml) boiling water

Per tablespoon: 130 calories, 15 g total fat, 2.5 g saturated fat, 0 g protein, 0 g carbohydrates, 0 g dietary fiber, 75 mg sodium

Mix the olive and sesame oils. Place the egg yolks in a food processor and process briefly. With the motor running, gradually add the oil in a slow, steady stream until it is all incorporated and the mixture has emulsified. Blend in the salt.

With the motor running, add the boiling water to stabilize the mayonnaise. Transfer to a jar with a tight-fitting lid and refrigerate until needed.

BEEF TENDERLOIN WITH PARSNIP MASH

The combination of beef and parsnip makes a real comfort food. It is worth buying smaller amounts of quality cuts of meat that contain less amounts of dense saturated fats. Serve with Balsamic Roast Beets (page 155) and some steamed carrots.

SERVES 4

10	medium parsnips
	Pinch of kosher salt
½	cup (120 ml) fat-free milk
½	teaspoon ground cumin
	Pinch of ground nutmeg
3	tablespoons fresh thyme leaves
1	tablespoon ground star anise
1	teaspoon pink peppercorns
8	pieces beef fillet, cut from the thinner tail end, 2.8 ounces (80 g) each
8	pancetta slices, sliced thinly
	Extra-virgin olive oil

Per serving: 550 calories, 14 g total fat, 4 g saturated fat, 39 g protein, 70 g carbohydrates, 15 g dietary fiber, 480 mg sodium

Peel the parsnips, cut lengthwise, remove the woody core, and coarsely chop. Bring a saucepan of salted water to a boil and cook the parsnips for 12 to 15 minutes, until tender. Drain, reserving ½ cup (120 ml) of the cooking liquid.

Place the empty saucepan over low heat and add the milk, cumin, and nutmeg. Return the parsnips to the pan and mash until smooth, adding a little cooking liquid if required.

Using a mortar and pestle, grind together the thyme, star anise, and peppercorns. Transfer to a plate and roll each piece of beef in the mixture. Encircle each piece with a slice of pancetta, using a toothpick to secure.

Heat a grill pan until hot over medium-high heat and brush with oil. Sear the beef in the pan until browned and cooked as desired, 3 minutes per side for medium. Let rest for 4 minutes before serving with the parsnip mash.

RENAISSANCE STEAK

During the Renaissance, there was, of course, no refrigeration, and so pickling the meat was a way of preserving it. In this recipe, which has been handed down for generations, the long marinating time allows many powerful ingredients to penetrate the steak: The acid in balsamic vinegar doesn't just flavor the meat, it also breaks down connective tissues, making the meat tender. I like to serve the steak with roasted potatoes and fresh ripe sliced tomatoes.

SERVES 4

½	cup (120 ml) extra-virgin olive oil
⅓	cup (80 ml) balsamic vinegar
2	tablespoons (30 g) green pickle relish
10	black peppercorns
1	tablespoon fresh oregano or ½ teaspoon dried
8	whole cloves
4	bay leaves
4	pieces shell steak, 1 inch (2.5 cm) thick, about 1¾ pounds (790 g)
1	cup Basic Bread Crumbs (page 159) or good-quality store-bought

Per serving: 490 calories, 26 g total fat, 8 g saturated fat, 48 g protein, 12 g carbohydrates, 0 g dietary fiber, 230 mg sodium

In a large shallow glass dish, combine the oil, vinegar, relish, peppercorns, oregano, cloves, and bay leaves. Add the steak and turn to coat the pieces. Cover and refrigerate overnight. In the morning remove from the refrigerator, turn the steak, cover, and return to marinate for 2 to 3 hours more, or until evening.

Preheat the broiler or heat a grill to high.

Spread the bread crumbs evenly on a sheet of parchment paper. Remove the steak from the marinade and place on top of the bread crumbs, turning to coat the pieces; discard the marinade. Transfer the meat to a rimmed baking sheet. Place under the broiler and cook for 6 minutes. Remove the tray from the broiler, place the steaks on a platter, and very carefully drain any fat from the tray into a metal tin. Return the steak to the pan, cooked side down, and cook for 6 to 8 minutes for medium-rare.

CHINESE SPARERIBS

An essential recipe for any household, ribs evoke memories of fun gatherings with family and friends. Baked in the oven, these ribs are as delicious as any cooked at a barbecue and are a treat served with fresh corn.

SERVES 6

1/3	cup (80 ml) ketchup
1/4	cup (60 ml) dry sherry
1/4	cup (60 ml) low-sodium soy sauce
3	tablespoons (45 ml) honey
1	tablespoon peeled and grated fresh ginger
1	garlic clove, peeled and crushed
1	teaspoon kosher salt
1	teaspoon freshly ground black pepper
2	slabs baby back ribs, about 4 pounds (2 kg) each

Per serving: 590 calories, 44 g total fat, 16 g saturated fat, 31 g protein, 14 g carbohydrates, 0 g dietary fiber, 980 mg sodium

In a medium bowl, mix the ketchup, sherry, soy sauce, honey, ginger, garlic, salt, and pepper.

Place the ribs in a single layer in a large baking dish and pour the marinade over them; turn to coat the pieces. Cover and refrigerate for 8 hours, turning occasionally.

Remove the ribs from the refrigerator 15 minutes before cooking.

Preheat the oven to 350°F (180°C). Reserving the marinade, transfer the ribs to a rimmed baking sheet. Cover and roast for 1 hour. Uncover, brush with the reserved marinade, and bake for another 20 to 30 minutes, or until tender and brown. Discard any remaining marinade. Serve.

STEAMED VEAL AND PARSLEY WITH CRISPY ARTICHOKES

Steaming thin cuts of meat and pairing them with aromatic and flavorful combinations of fresh herbs and vegetables is a healthy way to cook meat without the use of fats and oils.

SERVES 4

ARTICHOKES

12	small artichokes, each 2–3 inches (5–7.5 cm) long
1	large lemon, cut into wedges
1	cup (240 ml) extra-virgin olive oil
	Kosher salt and freshly ground black pepper

VEAL

1	pound (450 g) thin veal cutlets, sliced in half
½	cup finely minced scallions (white part only)
½	cup finely chopped fresh flat-leaf parsley
2	fresh sage leaves, finely minced
	Finely grated zest and juice of 1 lemon
¼	cup (60 ml) red wine vinegar
2	tablespoons (30 ml) extra-virgin olive oil
	Kosher salt and freshly ground black pepper
	Lemon wedges

Per serving: 400 calories, 22 g total fat, 3.5 g saturated fat, 32 g protein, 24 g carbohydrates, 10 g dietary fiber, 380 mg sodium

For the artichokes: Using a serrated knife, slice ½ inch (1.3 cm) off the top of each artichoke and rub the cut surface with lemon. Cut away any tough outer leaves and clean around the base using a vegetable peeler; rub the cut surfaces with lemon as you work. Using a teaspoon, ease the leaves of the artichokes open and scrape out any hairy choke from the interior using a grapefruit knife.

Heat the oil in a medium saucepan over medium heat until hot but not smoking. Using tongs, lower one artichoke at a time, upside down, into the oil; push on the artichoke bottom to force the leaves open. Cook until golden and crisp on the outside, about 3 minutes; drain on paper towels. Season with salt and pepper. Keep warm.

For the veal: Place 1 inch (2.5 cm) of water in a large saucepan and bring to a simmer over medium heat. Place the veal in the steamer basket and lower into the saucepan. Cover and cook for 10 minutes, or until the veal is just cooked.

In a small bowl, mix the scallions, parsley, sage, and lemon zest. Remove the meat from the steamer and stack onto warm serving plates, sprinkling the scallion mixture between the layers.

In a small bowl, mix the lemon juice, vinegar, and oil. Drizzle over the meat. Season with salt and pepper. Serve the veal with the artichokes and lemon wedges.

IN PRAISE OF THE ARTICHOKE

A nice fat artichoke makes the most wonderful of appetizers. Because it takes so long to eat it, you feel quite satisfied by the time you are done with it. For this reason, my husband and I love to start dinner with this prickly delicacy. Not only does it give us a chance to relax at the beginning of a meal, it also curbs our appetite so that, perhaps, we do not eat as much later.

But for me, preparation is key. Before cooking an artichoke, I give it a good trim: I cut off the stem, and I also cut the top, almost halfway down, to get rid of the sharp barbs at the end of the leaves.

I drop the whole artichoke into boiling water and cook it until the heart is soft when pricked with a knife. Then I remove it and turn it upside down to drain out the water. After the artichoke has cooled down, I separate its leaves slightly, as if to open up the blossom of a flower.

Before serving, I clean out the choke with a serrated grapefruit knife.

BUTTERFLIED LEG OF LAMB WITH GIN AND JUNIPER BERRIES

An unusual marinade makes for the most tender meat. Have your butcher trim, split, and debone a whole leg of lamb for you. Even though the pineapple is discarded with the marinade, slicing some extra pineapple and grilling it to serve with the lamb makes a pretty presentation.

SERVES 6 TO 8

½ cup (120 ml) gin

½ cup (120 ml) unsweetened pineapple juice

12 juniper berries

3 bay leaves

1 boneless leg of lamb, 4–5 pounds (2–2.3 kg), trimmed

1 small ripe pineapple, peeled, cored, and sliced into ¼-inch (6 mm) rounds

Per serving (based on 8 servings): 480 calories, 31 g total fat, 14 g saturated fat, 42 g protein, 1 g carbohydrates, 0 g dietary fiber, 170 mg sodium

In a large glass baking dish or roasting pan, combine the gin, pineapple juice, juniper berries, and bay leaves. Add the lamb, unfolded, and arrange the pineapple slices over the meat. Cover and refrigerate for at least 4 hours or overnight.

Remove the pineapple slices to a plate and turn the lamb in the marinade; replace the pineapple slices. Cover and return to the refrigerator for 2 hours; remove 30 minutes before grilling.

Preheat a grill to high. Oil the grill grate. Place the lamb on the grill; discard the marinade and pineapple. Cook for 15 minutes on each side until the desired doneness is reached and a minimum internal temperature of 145°F (63°C) is achieved. Transfer the meat to a serving platter and allow it to rest for 20 minutes before slicing and serving.

NOTE: To roast the lamb indoors, preheat the oven to 400°F (200°C). Cut the lamb in half to fit onto two large cast-iron grill skillets. Cook over high heat for 8 minutes. Flip the pieces, reduce the heat to medium-high, and cook for 13 minutes. Transfer to a baking dish and bake for 10 minutes.

LA TULIPE'S
APRICOT SOUFFLÉ

This dessert was inspired by La Tulipe, a now-defunct restaurant in New York. The natural sugar of the apricots is almost all that is required to sweeten this velvety soufflé.

SERVES 7

1	pound (450 g) dried apricots
4	cups (960 ml) cold water
	Juice of ½ lemon
½	cup superfine (caster) sugar, plus extra for the ramekins
	Butter for ramekins
7	large egg whites, at room temperature
	Pinch of salt

Per serving: 260 calories, 1.5 g total fat, 0.5 g saturated fat, 6 g protein, 55 g carbohydrates, 3 g dietary fiber, 110 mg sodium

Combine the apricots and 3 cups (720 ml) of the water in a medium saucepan. Allow to stand for 2 hours. Add the remaining 1 cup (240 ml) water and bring to a boil over high heat. Reduce the heat to low, cover, and simmer for 20 minutes.

Transfer the apricots and half of the liquid to a food processor. Add the lemon juice and ¼ cup of the sugar; process until smooth and the consistency of thick applesauce. (If the mixture seems too thick, add a bit more cooking liquid.) Transfer 2 cups of the puree to a medium bowl and cool to room temperature. Reserve the remaining puree for the sauce.

Preheat the oven to 375°F (190°C). Lightly butter seven 1-cup (240 ml) ramekins or a 6-cup (1.5 liter) soufflé dish and coat the interior with sugar.

Place the egg whites and salt in a large bowl. Beat with a hand-held electric mixer until soft peaks form. Gradually beat in the remaining ¼ cup sugar and continue to beat until stiff but not dry. Stir one-quarter of the egg whites into the apricot puree and then gently fold the puree into the remaining whites. Spoon into the ramekins or soufflé dish. Bake for 20 to 30 minutes, until puffed and golden. Serve with the remaining apricot puree.

POACHED PEARS IN RED WINE

My husband adores pears, and this is a lovely light dessert to have after any meal, although it is particularly delicious after Signature Roast Duck (page 192). I sometimes cool the syrup and stir in 1 tablespoon (15 g) of vanilla ice cream for every ¼ cup (60 ml) of syrup to make an extra-special sauce. For variety, you can substitute white wine for the red, and often, I peel the pears with a lemon zester, which makes an interesting striped design.

SERVES 4

3	cups (720 ml) dry red wine
1	cup sugar
1	vanilla bean
1	cinnamon stick
4	small firm ripe pears, peeled
4	top sprigs fresh mint

Per serving (1 pear with 2 tablespoons syrup): 250 calories, 0 g total fat, 0 g saturated fat, 1 g protein, 49 g carbohydrates, 4 g dietary fiber, 0 mg sodium

In a large nonstick skillet, combine the wine, sugar, vanilla bean, and cinnamon stick. Bring to a boil over medium-high heat, stirring constantly to dissolve the sugar. Reduce the heat to medium and add the pears. Simmer, uncovered, for 15 minutes, or until the pears are soft but not mushy when pierced with sharp knife.

Cool the pears in the syrup until lukewarm; discard the vanilla bean and cinnamon stick. Transfer the pears to individual dessert plates with a slotted spoon. Spoon the syrup over the pears and serve garnished with the mint.

WALDORF CHOCOLATE MOUSSE

This recipe from Chef Jean-Claude Perennou at the Waldorf-Astoria Hotel was created for The Breast Cancer Research Foundation symposium in October 2005. It is a chocolate lovers' dream come true and was so popular that we had to publish it in our Spring newsletter.

SERVES 6

8	ounces (230 g) Valrhona Manjari chocolate or other bittersweet chocolate
2	tablespoons (30 g) butter
7	large egg whites, at room temperature
3	tablespoons sugar

Per serving: 270 calories, 20 g total fat, 10 g saturated fat, 7 g protein, 28 g carbohydrates, 3 g dietary fiber, 90 mg sodium

Melt the chocolate and butter in a double boiler or in a metal bowl set over a pan of simmering water, stirring frequently. Remove and set aside to cool.

In a separate bowl, combine the egg whites and sugar. Beat with a hand-held electric mixer until the egg whites hold stiff peaks.

Fold the whites into the melted chocolate and spoon into individual dessert bowls or a larger decorative bowl. Refrigerate for several hours before serving.

FAMOUS ORANGE DESSERT

It is not terribly complicated to make, but my family loves this cake-and-fruit combination, and I hope you will, too. If you need to save time, you can make the cake a day ahead or buy an angel food cake from a local bakery.

SERVES 8

CAKE

1½	cups sugar
1	cup cake flour, sifted
10	large egg whites, at room temperature
2	tablespoons (30 ml) warm water
1	teaspoon cream of tartar
1	teaspoon (5 ml) orange extract
¼	teaspoon salt

ORANGES

9	navel oranges
1	jar (6 ounces/170 g) coarse-cut marmalade
¼	cup (60 ml) orange juice
1	tablespoon (15 ml) Cointreau, Triple Sec, or Grand Marnier (optional)

Per serving: 350 calories, 0 g total fat, 0 g saturated fat, 7 g protein, 82 g carbohydrates, 4 g dietary fiber, 140 mg sodium

For the cake: Preheat the oven to 350°F (180°C).

Place the sugar in a food processor and process for 2 minutes, until superfine. Sift half of the sugar with the flour; set the remaining sugar aside.

In a large bowl, combine the egg whites, water, cream of tartar, orange extract, and salt. Beat using a hand-held electric mixer until firm peaks form, about 4 minutes. Gradually beat in the reserved sugar until the mixture is glossy and forms stiff peaks, about 1 minute. Gradually fold in the flour mixture, one-third at a time; do not overmix.

Transfer to an ungreased 10-inch (25 cm) angel food pan with a removable base. Bake for 40 to 45 minutes, until the cake springs back when the top is lightly touched.

Balance the pan upside down on top of a sturdy bottle, to prevent decompression while cooling. When cool, run a knife around the edge of the pan and invert onto a plate.

For the oranges: Using a very sharp knife, remove all the skin and white pith from the oranges. Working over a bowl to catch the juices, slide the knife down one side of each fruit seg-

ment, then cut down the other side. Gently pull out the segment and place in a bowl. Squeeze the juice from the pith to the bowl with the segments.

Heat the marmalade, orange juice, and Cointreau, Triple Sec, or Grand Marnier (if using) in a small saucepan over medium heat, stirring to remove any lumps. Pour the warm mixture over the oranges, stirring to combine, and refrigerate until needed. To serve, pour the oranges over the cake and cut into slices.

BAKED NECTARINES IN RASPBERRY SAUCE

I eat out frequently, and so I often re-create at home healthy versions of meals I have enjoyed at restaurants. This is my interpretation of a dessert I sampled at Sette Mezzo in New York.

SERVES 4

4	ripe nectarines, halved and stone removed
8	amaretti cookies
8	teaspoons (40 ml) amaretto liqueur
1	pint raspberries
1	tablespoon sugar

Per serving: 240 calories, 7 g total fat, 1 g saturated fat, 4 g protein, 39 g carbohydrates, 7 g dietary fiber, 50 mg sodium

Preheat the oven to 375°F (190°C). Using a small teaspoon, take each nectarine half and scrape any pith from where the pit was removed.

Put the cookies into the bowl of a food processor and pulse to make small crumbs. Place the cookie crumbs into a small bowl, add the amaretto, and mix with a fork. Fill the nectarine halves with the mixture and place in an oven-proof dish. Bake for 15 to 20 minutes.

Press the raspberries through a fine sieve to remove the seeds. Heat the resulting juice in a small saucepan and stir in the sugar; simmer over medium heat for 7 minutes, or until the sauce has thickened. Drizzle a little raspberry sauce on each plate and place 2 nectarine halves on top. Serve.

MENUS

BREAKFAST FOR TWO
Bill Lieberman's Yogurt Shake

"Over the Top" Scrambled Eggs

FAMILY BREAKFAST
Almond Milk and Peach Smoothies

My Secret Recipe for Pancakes

Toasted Grain and Nut Sundaes with Berries

BRUNCH FOR FRIENDS
Every Berry Smoothies

Breakfast in a Muffin

The Most Delicious Fruit Salad, Ever

Gravlax

LIGHT LUNCH
Pomegranate with Lime, Low-Fat Ricotta, and Honey

Borscht Ring

Oven-Poached Lemon Chicken

Poached Leeks with Walnut Vinaigrette

Almond Milk Blancmange with Poached Peaches

LUNCH WITH FRIENDS
Gazpacho

Smoked Trout Salad a la Grècque

Potato Salad

Cheesecake with Chocolate Cookie Crust

WINTER LUNCH
Roasted Tomato Soup

Thyme and Honey Roast Pork with Beans

Black Rice Pudding with Banana "Ice Cream"

CASUAL DINNER FOR TWO
Spiced Pomegranate Sparkler

Red Snapper with Fennel

Brussels Sprouts with Orange and Chili

Baked Nectarines in Raspberry Sauce

DINNER WITH COMPANY
Baby Bellini

Broccoli Soup

Signature Roast Duck

Pureed Sweet Potatoes

Wild Rice with Dried Cherries and Nuts

Steamed Vegetable Medley with Bread Crumbs

Poached Pears in Red Wine

DINNER WITH FAMILY
Asian Pear, Fennel, and Jícama Salad

The Best Roast Chicken

Balsamic Roast Beets

Herbed Puy Lentils

Mock Snowflake "Potatoes"

Famous Orange Dessert

RESOURCE GUIDE

With thanks to the following retailers who were so generous in lending their merchandise for the photography in this book.

BACCARAT
625 Madison Avenue
New York, NY 10022
Phone: 212-826-4100

BERNARDAUD
499 Park Avenue
New York, NY 10021
Phone: 212-371-4300

CALVIN KLEIN
654 Madison Avenue
New York, NY 10021
Phone: 212-292-9000

H GROOME
9 Main Street
Southampton, NY 11968
Phone: 631-204-0491

LA CAFETIERE
160 9th Avenue
New York, NY 10011
Phone: 646-486-0667

MOSER
21440 Pacific Boulevard
Sterling, VA 20167
Phone: 866-240-5115

NICOLE FARHI
10 East 60th Street
New York, NY 10022
Phone: 212-223-8811

THE PORCELAIN ROOM
13 Christopher Street
New York, NY 10014
Phone: 212-367-8206

RIEDEL
95 Mayfield Avenue
Edison, NJ 08818
Phone: 732-346-8960

TAKASHIMAYA
693 5th Avenue
New York, NY 10022
Phone: 212-350-0100

INDEX

Boldface page references indicate photographs. *Italic* references indicate boxed text.